The Macintosh Bible Guide
to SYSTEM 7

*The Macintosh Bible Guide
to* SYSTEM 7

CHARLES RUBIN

*The most dramatic
changes ever in the
Mac's system software*

Goldstein & Blair • Box 7635 • Berkeley, California 94707

Additional copies of *The Macintosh Bible Guide to System 7* are available from Goldstein & Blair, Box 7635, Berkeley CA 94707, 510/524-4000. Single copies cost $12 plus $4 for shipping and tax (if any) to US addresses. (For information on other products, and shipping rates to foreign addresses, see the order pages in the back of the book.) We offer quantity discounts to computer stores, other retailers and wholesalers (except bookstores and book wholesalers), user groups, businesses, schools and individuals. Distribution to the book trade is through Publishers Group West, Box 8843, Emeryville CA 94662, 510/658-3453 (toll-free: 800/365-3453).

Goldstein & Blair donates at least 10%—last year, 11%—of its aftertax profits to organizations working for social justice.

Technical editing: John Kadyk, Alan Winslow, Susan McCallister, Todd Corleto
Copy-editing: Christine Carswell, John Kadyk, Susan McCallister, Alan Winslow
Proofreading: Karen Faria, Christine Carswell, John Kadyk, Susan McCallister
Index: Ty Koontz   Word processing: Jan Brenner
Cover design and art: Chris Molé   Cover concept: Arthur Naiman
Inside design: Anise Morrow, Arthur Naiman
Page layout (using PageMaker 4.0): Anise Morrow
Fonts: Univers, Janson Text (from Adobe)
Printing: Michelle Selby, Consolidated Printers, Berkeley CA

Library of Congress Cataloging-in-Publication Data

Rubin, Charles, 1953-
    The Macintosh Bible guide to System 7 : the most dramatic changes
ever in the Mac's system software / Charles Rubin.
      p. cm.
    Includes index.
    ISBN 0-940235-21-8 : $12.00
    1. Operating systems (Computers) 2. System 7. 3. Macintosh
(Computer)--Programming. I. Title.
QA76.76.063R82 1991
005.4'469--dc20   91-13742
                                                                                                     CIP

Copyright © 1991 by Charles Rubin. All rights reserved.

No part of this book may be reprinted, or reproduced, or utilized in any form or by any electronic, mechanical or other means, now known or hereafter invented, including photocopying and recording, or in any information storage and retrieval system, without prior permission in writing from the publisher.

printed in the United States of America   printing #   3 4 5 6 7 8 9

Table of Contents

Acknowledgements 6
Introduction 7

I GETTING STARTED
   1. System 7 at a glance **11**
   2. Installing System 7 **19**
   3. Starting up **33**

II THE FINDER AND ITS MENUS
   4. Working with the Finder **40**
   5. File and Edit menu commands **59**
   6. View, Label, Special, Help and Application menu commands **76**

III THE NEW SYSTEM FOLDER
   7. The System Folder **89**
   8. Using control panels **103**

IV WORKING WITH APPLICATIONS
   9. Using applications **121**
   10. Printing **139**

V SHARING FILES AND LINKING PROGRAMS
   11. File sharing **161**
   12. Users, groups, and access privileges **179**
   13. File sharing tips and troubleshooting **195**
   14. Program linking **203**

Glossary 211
Index 221

Each chapter also has a more detailed table of contents on its title page.

Acknowledgements

I'd like to thank the entire hard-working, fun-loving gang at Goldstein & Blair for their encouragement, insight and effort during the preparation of this book.

In particular, John Kadyk, Christine Carswell, Susan McCallister and Todd Corleto offered valuable comments on an early draft. John, Christine, Susan and Alan Winslow teamed up to edit the final manuscript.

John Grimes, Goldstein & Blair's sales director, is better at selling books than anyone I've met in the computer book business, so I'm thanking him in advance for his efforts on behalf of this one.

I'm also grateful to Arthur Naiman for suggesting this project to me, and for his excellent advice about the book's organization and focus.

The book's technical accuracy owes a lot to Barry Semo, author of the fabulous INITPicker program ($70 from Microseeds in Tampa, Florida) and contract programmer at Apple Computer. Barry straightened me out on several technical aspects of System 7, and did so under a very tight deadline. Any remaining mistakes, however, are my responsibility alone.

Trademark notice: Because one purpose of this book is to describe and comment on various products, many such products are identified by their tradenames. In most—if not all—cases, these designations are claimed as legally protected trademarks by the companies that make the products. It is not our intent to use any of these names generically, and the reader is cautioned to investigate a claimed trademark before using it for any purpose except to refer to the product to which it is attached. In particular: Apple and Macintosh are registered trademarks of Apple Computer, Inc. The Macintosh Bible is a trademark of Goldstein & Blair, which is not affiliated with Apple Computer, Inc.

Disclaimer: We've got to make a disclaimer that common sense requires: Although we've tried to check all the procedures described in this book to make sure they work as described, we can't guarantee that they do. Don't try anything except on a backup file. Satisfy yourself that the technique you're trying works before using it on your valuable files. We can't be—and aren't—responsible for any damage or loss to your data or your equipment that results directly or indirectly from your use of this book. We make no warranty, express or implied, about the contents of this book, its merchantability or its fitness for any particular purpose. The exclusion of implied warranties is not permitted by some states. The above exclusion may not apply to you. This warranty provides you specific legal rights. There may be other rights that you may have which vary from state to state.

Introduction

It's the system software that makes the Macintosh unique, and System 7 brings the most revolutionary changes to the Mac's software since it was introduced in 1984. It makes using Macs even easier and a lot more powerful. Soon very few Mac users will be without it.

Every new Macintosh now comes with System 7 and a set of manuals for it. If you bought your Mac before System 7 came out in May 1991, the chances are you'll want to upgrade. System 7 requires at least two megabytes of RAM and a hard disk to run, but once you see what it can do, the cost and/or hassle of upgrading your Mac will seem trivial compared to the power you'll gain.

Who this book is for

This book is primarily for people upgrading to System 7 from previous versions of the Mac system software. Since you're already familiar with the Mac, we'll get you up to speed quickly by focusing on what's new and different in System 7, rather than wasting your time rehashing mouse-clicking and other basic Mac features.

Apple's official System 7 product and manuals cost $100 (as of this writing, anyway). But you can take a few floppy disks down to your Apple dealer and get a free copy of the System 7 software, and then buy this book. The $90 you save will probably buy a couple of extra megabytes of RAM for your Mac. Even if you bought a Mac after System 7 came out and thus have Apple's own manuals, you're likely to find this book more concise, more readable and better organized.

What this book assumes

Since *The Macintosh Bible Guide* assumes you've used a Mac before, it doesn't belabor the obvious and supposes you know how to use the Finder, windows, menus, icons and basic dialog boxes. Specifically, it assumes that you know how to:

- open a file, folder or disk
- save or print a file
- delete a file
- close a window
- resize or scroll a window or scroll a list in a dialog box
- choose a menu command
- use checkboxes and buttons
- press the [Return] or [Enter] key to select a heavily-outlined button in a dialog box (like the *OK* button) instead of clicking it
- quit a program
- move fonts and DAs using Font/DA Mover

If you've used a Mac for any time at all, you already understand most or all of these things (and the descriptions in this book are generous enough to make up for any minor gaps in your knowledge). If you don't, look them up in your old Mac manual, use the guided tour disk that came with your Mac, or buy a good reference like *The Macintosh Bible*.

How this book is organized

I've divided the book into five sections:

Section I, *Getting started*, takes you through upgrading, installing System 7 and starting up.

Section II, *The Finder and its menus*, covers the new desktop and menus.

Section III, *The new System Folder*, deals with the new control panel devices (now called control panels), new folders in the System Folder and new ways of installing fonts and utilities.

Section IV, *Working with applications*, covers new features like publishing, subscribing and stationery, as well as memory management and printing.

Section V, *Sharing files and linking programs*, deals with these powerful new network-related features of System 7.

In the back of the book, the glossary defines terms that are new in System 7, as well as others that may simply be unfamiliar to you. The index is a cross-reference for terms, concepts and procedures you'll use in System 7.

How to use the book

This book was designed to be read from beginning to end, but you'll probably end up picking out the chapters that interest you most. If you haven't installed System 7 yet, follow the instructions in Chapter 2 and then you'll be able to restart your Mac and poke around on your own.

The table of contents lists chapters, and each chapter has a title page that lists the sections within it so you can move quickly to topics that interest you. If you don't find what you're looking for there, check the index or glossary.

Conventions used in this book

Here are some conventions I've used in the interest of presenting information clearly and economically:

- System 6 and System 7 refer to all versions of these systems, while System 6.05 or System 7.0 (say) refer to the exact versions specified.

- Checking or unchecking a checkbox means clicking in it so an *X* appears or disappears (which selects or deselects the option the checkbox represents).

- The dialog boxes you see when you open the new control panel programs are called control panels instead of dialog boxes (because that's what Apple calls them).

To help you find your way through conventional dialog boxes, I show the names of the new dialog box areas, checkboxes and buttons, as well as new features generally, in **boldface** the first time they're explained, unless they're obvious buttons like *OK, Cancel* or *Quit.* Since *OK* and *Cancel* are universally understood, I don't bother explaining their functions—unless they do something remarkable in a particular case.

Since the screen illustrations in this book were taken from prerelease versions of System 7, some of them contain beta version numbers like 3.0b1. Your version of System 7 will show different version numbers.

Finally, I haven't documented trivial changes in the appearance of objects or alert boxes unless they affect the way you use the Mac.

The Mea Culpa department

I've done my best to present practical and readable descriptions of every System 7 feature without putting anyone to sleep. If you think there's a really hot tip that should be in here, or if you (gulp) discover a mistake, please write to me in care of Goldstein & Blair (the address is on the title page).

GETTING STARTED

Chapter 1
System 7 at a glance

What's new in System 7 **12**

System 6 features
 you won't find in System 7 **15**

What you need to run System 7 **16**

Should you upgrade? **17**

When it comes to improving the Mac, System 7 blows the doors off any previous change in the system software. It retains some basic features that go all the way back to 1984, but it also adds a lot of powerful new capabilities that will help the Mac keep its competitive edge through the 1990's.

As you might expect from a major increase in Mac capabilities, System 7.0 is not for every Mac user, and even if you *can* use it, you may not want to run right out and get it. In this chapter, I'll start with a quick look at System 7.0's new features. (Apple has planned even more features for future versions of System 7.) Then we'll see what hardware it takes to run System 7. Putting that information together will help you decide whether or not it's worth it to you to upgrade.

What's new in System 7

A more powerful, more flexible Finder

The new **Finder** makes your desktop easier to manage, with more control over how icons and windows look, easier access to applications and more ways to arrange items on the desktop.

It works like MultiFinder, which was an option with System 6. This means you can always have as many programs open as your Mac's memory allows and, if you have a PostScript printer like the Apple LaserWriter, you can print documents in the background while you do other work.

Easier font, sound and DA management

To install fonts, sounds and DAs, you just drag them into the System Folder. There's no more Font/DA Mover program and no more fifteen-DA limit on the menu. To view fonts and play sounds, you just doubleclick them.

Built-in Help

There's a new **Help** menu in the Finder which explains parts of the desktop, windows and system software files as you point to them. You can also display a list of keyboard shortcuts.

System 7 comes with help information only for the Finder, but future developers will use this menu to add instant help to their own programs.

Aliases

Aliases are stand-ins for folders, disks, files or programs. Got a folder you work with all the time? Put aliases of it on the menu, on the desktop and in any other folder where you might need quick access to it.

Aliases don't take up a lot of disk space because they're not copies—they're just remote-control switches that permit you to open the real items they stand for.

Stationery

Some programs have a **stationery** option that lets you create letterheads, memo pages or other preformatted templates and then open them as new untitled documents. System 7 lets you make stationery for any program.

TrueType fonts

System 7's new **TrueType** fonts work both for printing and to display characters smoothly on the Mac screen, so you don't have to keep separate screen and printer versions of the same font. And you only need one file for a whole typeface like Helvetica (no more messing with Helvetica 10, 12 and 14). TrueType fonts can be used right along with any of your old fonts, even in the same document.

File sharing

File sharing lets you share data with other people on a network without having to buy special software like AppleShare or an electronic mail program. If your Mac is on a network, you can designate folders or disks on your system as shared items, so other people on the network can use them.

Virtual memory

Virtual memory tells your Mac to set aside free space on a hard disk as extra RAM. With the right Mac (see *What you need to run System* 7 below), virtual memory can double your RAM.

32-bit addressing

32-bit addressing (how the Mac manages memory) allows Mac IIci, IIfx, IIsi or LC owners to access far more RAM than those with other Macs (which are limited to the memory they can access with 24-bit addresses). Rather than being restricted to four or eight megabytes, these more advanced Macs can use from 10 to 128 megabytes of RAM. This will really help people who work with extra large graphics or spreadsheet files or who want to work with lots of big programs open at the same time.

Publish and subscribe

Publish and subscribe is a kind of automatic cut-and-paste function that lets you link documents created by different programs. For example, you can *publish* part of a spreadsheet and then *subscribe* to those published numbers in a word processor document. If you change the spreadsheet file, the spreadsheet numbers in the word processor document will automatically be updated.

(This feature must be incorporated into specific programs. Some programs will support it within a month or two of System 7's release.)

Program linking

Program linking allows programs to exchange information without your intervention. For example, a color paint program could ask a compression utility to compress or decompress its files as they are saved or opened; or a spreadsheet program could ask a word processing program to check a worksheet for spelling errors.

This feature must be supported by specific programs. Program linking is far more complex than publish and subscribe, and it will be several months after System 7's release before we see it supported by a significant number of Mac programs.

Data Access Language (DAL)

With **DAL** you'll be able to use your favorite spreadsheet or word processor program to get information from a network or mainframe database without having to know that database's specific query language.

Only the basic DAL facilities are included with System 7.0 (they're in a file inside the System Folder) and you won't find any further discussion of DAL in this book. Once developers begin supporting DAL, you'll be able to learn about it from their application manuals.

System 6 features you won't find in System 7

Some of the features and utility programs we've grown used to in System 6 have been eliminated from System 7, because they're not needed anymore or have been replaced by something better.

MacroMaker, the Apple-supplied keystroke macro program, isn't included with System 7 and won't work with it.

Font/DA Mover, the utility you needed to add fonts or DAs to the System file in previous versions of the system software, is also gone because it isn't needed anymore. You now install fonts by just dragging them into the System file, and DAs work like ordinary programs under System 7 (see Chapter 7).

The Access Privileges DA and *Get Privileges...* command you used under System 6 if you were an AppleShare user have now been replaced by the *Sharing...* command on the File menu (see Chapter 5).

The *Set Startup...* command is gone from the Special menu, because you can now set anything to open automatically at startup by dragging it inside System 7's Startup Items folder (see Chapter 7).

MultiFinder is gone, since its functions are performed by the System 7 Finder.

What you need to run System 7

System 7 requires at least two megabytes of RAM and a SCSI hard disk with at least three megabytes of free space on it. That's just to run the system software and work with one or two relatively small applications open at the same time (a word processor and a DA, perhaps). The more RAM and disk space you have, the better.

There's a definite hardware class structure to performance gains with System 7:

Left at the gate—Mac 128K, 512K, 512Ke models and any other Mac with one megabyte of RAM or without a SCSI hard disk. These can't run System 7 at all.

Coach—Mac Plus, SE, Portable and standard Mac II models can run System 7, but they can't use virtual memory or 32-bit addressing.

Business Class—The Mac LC can use up to 10 megabytes of RAM in 32-bit addressing mode, but can't use virtual memory.

First Class—Mac II's with PMMU chips, or the SE/30, Mac IIsi, IIx, IIcx, IIci or IIfx can use 65 megabytes (Mac IIsi) or 128 megabytes (other models) of RAM and can access up to 1 gigabyte of virtual memory. (The SE/30, Mac II, IIx and IIcx all require software like A/UX or Connectix Mode 32 to use virtual memory or System 7's 32-bit addressing mode.)

(I suppose someone out there will find a way to install System 7 on a high-density 1.44 megabyte floppy disk. But for this to work, you'd have to strip away a lot of the fonts, printer drivers and other extra files, and your Mac's performance would be far worse than when running System 6 from a floppy. Trying to shoehorn System 7 into less space than it was designed for is asking for trouble.)

Should you upgrade?

With the new features and the hardware realities of running System 7 fresh in mind, your decision to upgrade will be based on the state of your system and on your financial priorities.

If you're one of the millions who's only a one-megabyte memory upgrade away from System 7, all the new features are well worth the $50 (or less) per meg you'll have to spend for the extra RAM. Along with the new features, you'll be able to use all your old fonts and most of your existing inits, DAs, sounds and other system software add-ons.

If your system lacks a hard drive, you'll have to spend major bucks to make it compatible with System 7, but the performance leap from a floppy-driven Mac on System 6 to one running System 7 on a hard drive will knock your socks off. Still, if you're happy with your system, it may not be worth your trouble or expense to switch.

System 7 is a bigger, more complex collection of programs than System 6, and it takes more horsepower to run. On 68000-based Macs like the Plus, you may find that some operations take a little longer, but the extra features should make up for the slight lag.

Anyone familiar with previous Mac system upgrades will be leery of bugs in early versions of System 7. But even its prerelease versions were far less buggy than the first version of System 6, so you'll be able to use System 7.0 immediately with very few problems.

On the other hand, you aren't forced to upgrade just because others on your network are using System 7. Your System 6-based Mac can coexist on a network with System 7-based Macs as long as you upgrade your LaserWriter or other network printer drivers to the System 7 version. Otherwise, you'll be reinitializing the network printer every time you use it after someone on System 7.

GETTING STARTED

Chapter 2
Installing System 7

Do you need to use the Installer? **20**

The best way to install System 7 **20**

Installing from floppy disks **23**

Installing from a file server, or another local hard disk or CD-ROM disk **27**

If the installation fails **29**

When the Installer is finished **29**

Reclaiming disk space **32**

Do you need to use the Installer?

Yes, you do. Like every version of Mac system software, System 7 comes with an Installer program. In days gone by, you could install Mac system software more quickly by hand—you simply dragged the files from their floppy disks or another hard disk onto the destination disk. Don't even think of trying that now. Here's why:

- System 7's files (which fill several floppy disks) must be organized and assembled in the right places.

- The Installer automatically determines which model of Mac you have and installs a different version of System 7 accordingly.

The best way to install System 7

The best way to install System 7 is to put it on a disk that doesn't contain a System Folder. As we'll see, eliminating an existing System Folder isn't as hard as you might think.

Preparing your disk for installation

The only way the Installer or the Mac itself can identify a System Folder is by the System and Finder files inside it. These two files *bless* the System Folder, so the Mac will use its files to start up and run.

To turn your System Folder back into an ordinary folder, simply remove either the System or Finder file from it. After you *unbless* it this way, the System 7 Installer will ignore this folder and create a brand new System Folder during installation.

However, your existing System Folder probably has lots of files in it that you want to keep, including fonts, DAs, inits, control panel devices (cdevs) and program preferences files you installed yourself. You can move these files into the new System Folder once the System 7 Installer is finished.

Here's the procedure for preparing your disk for installation:

1. Restart your Mac with the Disk Tools disk from your set of System 7 floppy disks, or from another startup floppy. (You can't start up with the Install 1 disk because it will automatically run the Installer program and you're not ready to install the system software yet.)

2. If you've installed fonts, DAs or sounds directly in your System file and you don't have their original files stored elsewhere, drag the existing System file into a different folder. Once you've installed System 7, you can open the old System file and drag its fonts, sounds and DAs onto the new System Folder.

3. Drag the Finder file to the Trash and empty the Trash.

4. Rename your current System Folder *Stuff*, so you won't confuse it with the new System Folder.

5. Open the Stuff folder and delete all the standard Apple system software files (the System 7 Installer will install new versions). If you're not sure which are standard Apple system software files, they're listed below (your old System Folder probably won't contain all of them):

Access Privileges	Keyboard
AppleTalk	Laser Prep
AppleTalk ImageWriter	LaserWriter
AppleShare	LQ AppleTalk ImageWriter
Backgrounder	LQ ImageWriter
Battery	MacroMaker
Brightness	Monitors
Clipboard File	Map
CloseView	Mouse
Color	MultiFinder
DA Handler	Personal LaserWriter
Easy Access	PrintMonitor
Finder	Responder
Finder Startup	Scrapbook File
Font/DA Mover	Sound
General	Startup Device
ImageWriter	System
Key Layout	32-bit QuickDraw

Now there's no System Folder on your hard disk, all your custom system software files are saved in the Stuff folder and you're ready to install System 7.

Why you shouldn't replace an existing System Folder

Instead of the above procedure, you *can* replace an existing System Folder when you install System 7. This avoids having to copy your custom system software files into the new System Folder after installation. But it's not such a hot idea.

Because the System, Finder and other System Folder files are opened and closed a lot as you use your Mac, they can sustain minor damage from power surges, static electricity, cosmic rays (seriously!) and other problems. If you update an existing System Folder when you install System 7, you run the risk that damage in your System or Finder files will be "updated" to your System 7 software as it's installed. You might not notice any problems right away, but they could surface later on. Eliminating the System Folder from your disk and creating a new one removes the main risk of corrupted file problems—and since these problems tend to be very unpleasant, it's best to do what you can to avoid them.

(For the same reason, you should replace your System Folder files every few months as a precaution; this usually also cures minor problems you may have opening, saving or printing files.)

Installing from floppy disks

Here's how to install using floppy disks:

1. Copy the complete set of System 7 installation disks, put the originals away in a safe place and label your copies Install 1, Install 2, Install 3, Printing, Disk Tools, Fonts, Tidbits and More Tidbits, to match the original disks.

2. Restart your Mac with your copy of the Install 1 disk. You'll see an information screen that explains what the **Installer** does.

Click the *OK* button and you'll see the **Easy Install** dialog box, like this:

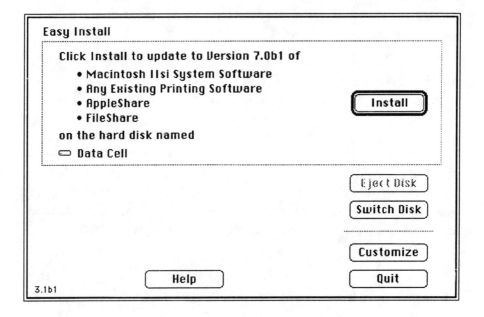

3. Check the name of the disk to make sure it's the one you want to install on. (The disk showing will probably be the Install 1 floppy you started up with. If so, you'll see a message saying you can't install System 7 on it.) Click the ***Switch Disk*** button until your hard disk's name is showing like the Data Cell name in the example above.

4. Next, you need to decide whether you want to use the Easy Install method or Customize your installation.

   The Easy Install option gives you the whole enchilada: all system software for your Mac, printer drivers for every Apple printer it can use, AppleShare user software and file-sharing software. To select Easy Install, click the ***Install*** button.

2. INSTALLING SYSTEM 7

The **Customize** option lets you order à la carte, selecting only the specific system resources you want installed. This option saves disk space by not installing printer and networking drivers you don't need now (you can also use it later, if you want to add an extra driver after you've installed System 7). To select this option, click the *Customize* button. You'll see a scrolling list of specific system resources you can install, like this:

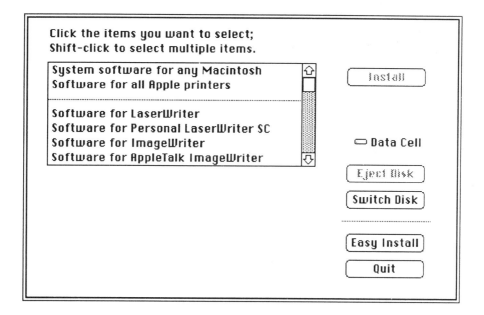

Click on the resource you want to install (Shift-click to select several resources). A description of each resource you select appears underneath the first list, like this:

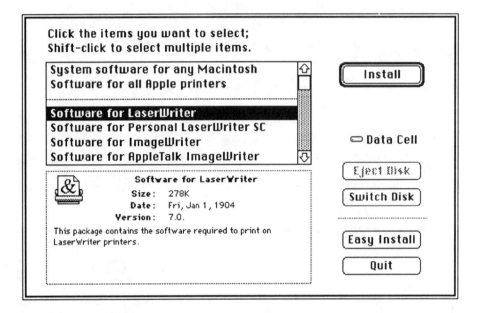

If you choose more than one resource, the resource names are displayed in a list. Once you've selected the resources you want installed, click the *Install* button.

5. You'll be prompted to insert various System 7 disks as the Installer needs files from them during the installation process.

If the installation is successful, you'll see a message saying so, with buttons to *Continue* or *Quit*. Clicking *Continue* returns you to the Easy Install screen so you can do other installations. Clicking *Quit* displays the shutdown screen, where you can either turn off your Mac or click the *Restart* button to start it up again. Once you restart, you'll be running under System 7.

If the installation wasn't successful, you'll see an explanatory message. See *If the installation fails* on p. 29 of this chapter.

Installing from a file server or another local hard disk or CD-ROM disk

If you're updating system software for several Macs on a network or if you just want to save yourself some floppy swapping, you can install System 7 from a file server, CD-ROM disk or another hard disk connected to your Mac. (Such a disk is called a *local* hard disk because it's in a SCSI chain connected directly to your Mac—a *file server*, by contrast, is a remote hard disk that's accessed across a Mac network.)

If you want to install from a CD-ROM disk, you must of course use one that contains the System 7 installation files. (You can also install from a file-sharing Mac, but this isn't really worth considering—to even *use* file sharing, you have to already be running System 7 on the Mac where you want to install it. And installing via file sharing is slower than from a local hard disk or file server.)

Putting Installer files on a local hard disk or file server

Before you can install from a local hard disk or file server, you need to load the System 7 installation files onto it:

1. Make a new folder on the hard disk or network server you'll be installing from and name it *Install Stuff*.

2. Insert each of the System 7 floppy disks into your disk drive and then drag its icon on top of the hard disk or network server icon. The Mac will copy each floppy disk's files into a folder with that floppy's name.

3. Drag each folder created from a System 7 floppy into the Install Stuff folder.

Installing from a file server

1. Create a startup floppy disk that contains enough system software to start up your Mac and log onto your file server. It

could be a squeeze fitting all the files you'll need to do this on an 800K floppy disk, but you can do it if you delete all the printer drivers, the Scrapbook file, any custom fonts and every DA except the Chooser and Control Panel from the System Folder and System file.

2. Restart your Mac from the new startup floppy and, if you haven't already, unbless your old System Folder using the procedure explained on p. 20, *Preparing your disk for installation.*

3. Log onto the file server.

4. Open the Install 1 folder inside the Install Stuff folder on the server, then open the Installer program there. You can then continue the installation following the steps described on p. 23, *Installing from floppy disks*, except that you won't have to swap floppies during the process.

Installing from a local hard disk or CD-ROM disk

To install from a local hard disk or CD-ROM disk, you should use that disk to start up your Mac. If it isn't the one that usually does this, you can make it the startup disk by following the procedure under *Switching startup disks* on p. 36, Chapter 3. Then:

1. Restart your Mac.

2. Prepare the disk where you'll be installing System 7 (if you haven't already done so—see *Preparing your disk for installation* on p. 20).

3. When you're ready to do the installation, open the Install 1 folder inside the Install Stuff folder and then open the Installer program there. You can then complete the installation following the steps outlined in *Installing from floppy disks* on p. 23, but without having to swap floppies during the process.

If the installation fails

If the installation isn't successful, you'll see a message that tells you why. It's usually because one of the files needed by the Installer is missing or damaged or there's something wrong with the hard disk where you're installing the new System Folder.

If the message says an Installer file or script is missing or damaged, make a new copy of the Installer files on your floppy disks, hard disk or network server and try the installation process again. If you get the same message, you may have a damaged version of the Installer files and will have to try a different set of Installer files from another source.

If the message says the hard disk isn't working properly or can't be located, try updating its driver using the setup software that came with it. (Don't reinitialize or reformat the hard disk unless you want to erase everything on it—just update the driver.) Then try the installation process again. If you still get a message that says the hard disk isn't working, back up all the data on the hard disk, reformat it and try the installation once more.

When the Installer is finished

Once the Installer has done its work and you've restarted your Mac, you're running under System 7.

If you updated an existing System Folder, System 7 will have moved all the old inits, DAs, cdevs and other system software files from the old System Folder to the new one.

If you installed System 7 using the best method, discussed at the beginning of this chapter, you'll have only the Apple-supplied system software, control panel files, printer drivers and networking files. It's now time to reinstall all the files you copied into the Stuff folder, and to move the fonts, DAs and sounds from your old System file (if any) to the new System folder. Your new, intelligent System Folder makes this easy to do:

1. Restart your Mac if you haven't already done so.

2. Open the disk icon for your startup disk and make the window big enough for you to see the System Folder and the Stuff folder at the same time.

3. Open the Stuff folder and select all the files and folders in it by pressing ⌘ A.

4. Drag the selected contents from the Stuff folder onto the new System Folder icon. An alert message will ask:

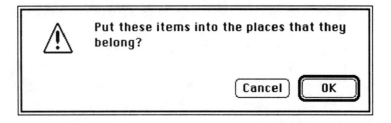

Note: This procedure works only if you drag files on top of the System Folder icon, not if you drag the files inside the open System Folder itself. If you drag a file or folder into the open System Folder, System 7 assumes you know what you're doing and doesn't attempt to examine file types or arrange the files accordingly. Fonts, sounds and some init files may not work properly unless they're inside the correct folder inside the System Folder.

5. Click the *OK* button. A dialog box will show you the progress of the files being copied. When they're all done, another dialog box will tell you where they were put, like this:

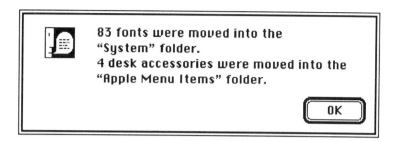

Some of your old system software files may not be properly identified and the System Folder won't know what to do with them. In this case, they'll simply be placed inside the System Folder itself.

6. Click the *OK* button.

When you drag font and DA suitcase files into the System Folder, System 7 automatically opens the suitcase files and installs fonts inside the System file and DAs inside the Apple Menu Items folder. After it does this, it automatically tries to delete the old suitcase files from inside the System Folder so they don't clutter it up. This isn't always possible, in which case you'll see a message like this:

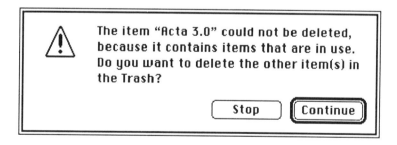

7. Click the *Continue* button if you want to toss out whatever else is in the Trash or the *Stop* button if you want to leave the Trash the way it is.

Now you can move any custom fonts, sounds and DAs from your old System file using basically the same procedure:

1. Locate your old System file and double-click on it to open its window. You'll see all the fonts, DAs and sounds installed in it.

2. Drag any fonts, DAs or sounds you want from the old System file's window onto the new System Folder icon. You'll see the same alert messages you did when you dragged from the Stuff folder. Click the *OK* button to install the files.

Note: Your old System file will contain some fonts, sounds and DAs that you don't need to copy because new versions of them have already been installed with the System 7 software. These include DAs like the Chooser, fonts like Geneva or sounds like Boing. Be sure you don't copy any of these standard fonts, sounds or DAs from your old System file.

Reclaiming disk space

Once you've installed everything, you can reclaim some disk space from your System Folder or elsewhere, especially if you used the Easy Install option.

For instance, from the System Folder you can delete any printer drivers that work with printers you don't use. This can easily save you a quarter of a megabyte or so since most printer drivers are from 40K to 100K in size.

Elsewhere on the disk, you can eliminate those utilities that have been upgraded in System 7 or aren't needed anymore. These include Apple File Exchange, Apple HD SC Setup, Disk First Aid, Font/DA Mover, LaserWriter Font Utility, CloseView and TeachText. You'll find new versions of all of these on one of the System 7 utilities disks.

GETTING STARTED

Chapter 3
Starting up

System software compatibility problems **34**

Starting up with more than one
hard disk connected **36**

The Desktop and Trash folders **38**

Opening files automatically at startup **38**

When you start your Mac up with System 7 installed, the procedure will be familiar: you'll see the "happy Mac" icon followed by the Welcome to Macintosh box and then the Finder desktop. But not all the inits, cdevs, DAs and other system software files you copied over to the new System Folder from your old one will work under System 7.

If you have problems starting from your hard disk under System 7, you'll need to use a floppy disk instead. The System 7 Disk Tools disk contains a stripped-down System Folder you can use to start up your Mac. (Again, don't try this with the Install 1 disk from the System 7 floppy disk set—it'll automatically load the Installer program.)

In this chapter we'll look at how to solve common startup problems, alternative ways to start your Mac and how to have programs automatically open when you turn it on.

System software compatibility problems

Startup incompatibilities

Most startup problems are caused by incompatibilities between System 7 and older inits or other programs on your disk. If you have such an incompatibility, you can locate it as follows:

1. Restart your Mac from your System 7 Disk Tools disk, but hold down [Shift] while you do so. This will prevent any init files (or **system extensions**, as they're called under System 7) from loading. If your Mac starts up fine, then one or more of the system extensions is probably the source of the trouble.

2. Open the System Folder on your hard disk and then open the Extensions folder inside it.

3. Drag all your old inits completely out of the System Folder. (Don't just drag them outside the Extensions folder and into

the System Folder, because the Mac may try to load them at startup again.) Check the Control Panels folder for init files too, and drag any inits in there outside the System Folder.

(Note: If you have INITPicker or another init management program, it's easier to turn your inits off with that instead of moving them.)

4. Restart the Mac from the hard disk. If it starts up fine, try reinstalling the inits inside the Extensions folder one at a time, restarting the Mac after each init, until you see which one(s) is (are) causing the problems. (Again, if you have an init management program, just use it to turn the inits back on.) Get rid of the problem inits—trash them or at least keep them out of the System Folder.

If your Mac still won't start up after you've removed all the old inits:

1. Update your hard disk's printer driver using whatever setup software came with the hard disk—the Apple HD SC Setup if it's one of Apple's disks.

2. Try reinstalling the system software again.

If these remedies fail, consult your local computer guru or Apple dealer.

Running incompatibilities

Once you have System 7 running, try out all your old inits, control panel files, DAs and FKey programs one at a time. Some may cause the Mac to display a message telling you the program doesn't work. Others may simply cause your Mac to crash.

If a program doesn't work properly, it's probably incompatible and it's best not to use it. If you really don't want to give up such a program, call the manufacturer and explain your problem—there may be a new version that works with System 7.

Starting up with more than one hard disk connected

If you have more than one hard disk connected to your Mac and each has a System Folder, you can choose which to use as the startup disk.

Startup disk scanning order

Normally, the startup disk is determined by the SCSI scanning order. The Mac searches the various storage devices connected to it, looking for a System Folder to start up with. This is the sequence:

- First the Mac looks in any internal or external floppy drives.
- Next it looks on the internal hard disk (if any).
- Finally it looks on external hard disks.

Each hard disk has a unique SCSI address from 0 to 6. To choose among external hard disks, the Mac looks first at the one with the highest numbered address, then at those with lower numbers. Each SCSI hard disk must have a unique address or the Mac will get confused and probably won't start up at all.

(The Mac can't "see" external hard disks unless they're turned on and warmed up, so you should turn on any external hard disks a few seconds before you turn on your Mac to start it up.)

If you've just installed System 7 on one of two or more hard disks connected to your Mac, you may need to switch the startup disk to the one containing the System 7 software.

Switching startup disks

If you want your Mac to start up from a hard disk that wouldn't normally be first under the sequence shown above, you can use a control panel to designate a different one. Here's how to change the startup disk:

1. Open the Control Panels folder inside the System Folder.

2. Doubleclick on the Startup Disk icon. You'll see a control panel like this:

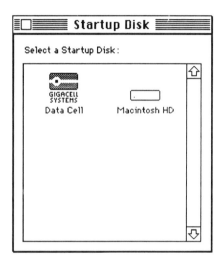

3. Click on the icon representing the startup disk you want.

Unless you reset the startup disk again, your Mac will start up from this disk from now on.

Note: In older versions of the system software, you could switch control of the Mac from the System file on one startup disk to the System file on another by holding down the ⌘ and Option keys and doubleclicking the System file you wanted to switch to, rather than restarting the Mac. This *does not work* under System 7.

The Desktop and Trash folders

System 7 creates two invisible folders—the **Desktop folder** and the **Trash folder**—on each disk whose icon appears on the desktop. The Mac uses these folders to keep track of files located on the desktop and in the Trash. If you then restart your Mac using System 6 or earlier software, both folders become visible. *Don't move or delete either folder*, particularly if there are files in them. If you delete these folders, you'll delete the files they contain (although the folders themselves will be replaced the next time you start up with System 7).

Opening files automatically at startup

Although the Mac normally starts up with the Finder, you can set it to start up and automatically load one or more additional programs, documents, DAs or control panels. Anything you set to load automatically this way is called a **startup item**.

In older versions of the system software, you used the *Set Startup...* command on the Finder's Special menu to designate startup items. Under System 7, this has been replaced by the Startup Items folder in the System Folder (see *The Startup Items folder* in Chapter 7, p. 98).

Using aliases as startup items

If you transfer documents or programs to the Startup Items folder, you'll have to navigate to that folder—way down inside the System Folder—whenever you want to open them from the desktop. Normally, it'd be more convenient to store these things at a higher level on the disk.

But in fact, you don't have to choose between making startup items and leaving a program or document in a convenient place on your disk.

You can create an alias and place *it* inside the Startup Items folder, keeping the real document or program stored in a more logical place. (For more on aliases, see *The Make Alias command* on p. 66 of Chapter 5.)

THE FINDER AND ITS MENUS

Chapter 4
Working with the Finder

Familiar features, subtle changes **41**

The Finder works like MultiFinder **42**

Managing program memory **43**

Printing in the background **44**

Icon cosmetics **45**

Window changes **46**

Other file management changes **49**

FKeys **52**

Keyboard shortcuts **54**

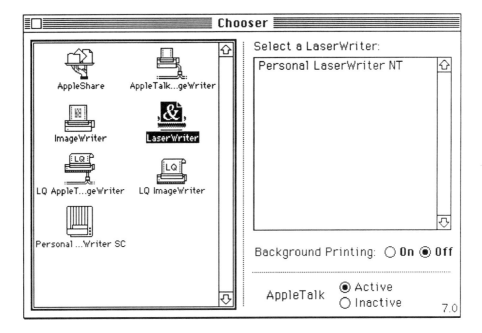

3. Click on the name of the LaserWriter you want to use, and then click the *On* button for background printing. After this, background printing will remain on until you turn it off.

For more information about background printing, see Chapter 10, p. 147.

Icon cosmetics

If your Mac's monitor can display 16 or more colors or shades of gray, and it's set to do that, the icons on the desktop have a shaded, three-dimensional effect. (To set your monitor to display colors or shades of gray, choose *Control Panels* from the menu, then doubleclick the Monitors icon inside the Control Panels folder. If your system is capable of this feature, you can turn it on in the Monitors control panel.)

If you have a color system, you can use System 7's Label menu to change the color of any icon on the desktop so you can manage files and folders more easily. Unlike System 6's Color menu, the Label menu's colors can be changed to any of the colors available in the Mac's color palette. (See *The Label menu*, Chapter 6, p. 77 for more information.)

System 7 also lets you replace icons with your own graphics (see *The Get Info* command in Chapter 5, p. 61).

Window changes

The Finder's windows behave a little differently under System 7. Let's look at the changes by working our way from the edges of a typical window toward the middle, starting with the title bar.

You'll see the window title, close box and zoom box in the title bar as before, but the title and zoom box work differently.

Pop-up window path

When you hold down ⌘ and click on a window's title in the Finder, you'll see a pop-up menu showing that window's directory path, like this:

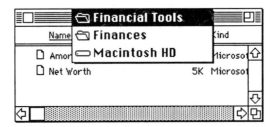

Hold down the mouse button and you can drag down this menu to select any other folder or the disk on the directory path to open or activate its window in the Finder.

Zoom works better

Clicking the zoom box now makes a window just large enough to show everything it contains. (Under System 6, the window opened to its maximum size, even if it contained only one item, often obscuring everything else on your desktop.)

As with System 6, clicking the zoom box a second time returns the window to its previous size.

New information, new ways to sort

The list view windows now include a new **Label** category so you can sort by item labels. (This new category—which you can see between the Kind and Last Modified columns in the example below—replaces the old Color sort category on color Macs.) By selecting an item and choosing one of seven labels from the Label menu in the Finder, you can put documents or folders into different categories. You can easily change the names and colors of labels with the Labels control panel (see *The Label menu* in Chapter 6, p. 77).

Name	Size	Kind	Label	Last Modified
▷ ☐ Consulting Invoices	—	folder	—	Wed, Jan 16, 19
☐ CWInvoice1/22/91	3K	Microsoft Word doc...	—	Fri, Jan 18, 19
☐ CWInvoice1/30/91	3K	Microsoft Word doc...	—	Wed, Jan 30, 1
☐ CWInvoice10/10	3K	Microsoft Word doc...	—	Fri, Oct 26, 19
☐ CWInvoice10/25	3K	Microsoft Word doc...	—	Fri, Oct 26, 19
☐ Invoice	3K	Microsoft Word doc...	—	Fri, Nov 9, 199

To quickly see how a list view window is sorted, look for the column heading that's underlined. (For example, the window above is sorted by item name.) To sort on a different category, just click on that category name.

Outline view

More importantly, list views can have an outline structure that shows several organizational levels of your disk at once. Here's how this works.

Notice the triangle next to the folder in the window above. If you click this triangle, the folder's contents will appear in a list immediately below it in the current window, like this:

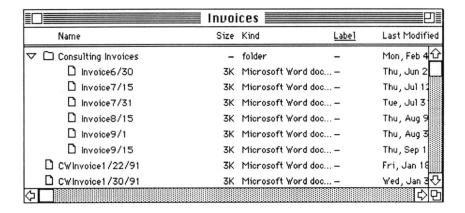

Now you are looking at items from two different organizational levels in the same window. (To indicate this, the triangle now points down instead of to the right.)

You can also select items from inside and outside a folder at the same time, like this:

Selecting groups of items in list views

Another nice change to the list views in System 7 is being able to drag the pointer across several folders or documents to select them as a group. Try it and see. (Before System 7, [Shift]-clicking was the only practical way to select more than one item in a text view window.)

Customizing window layouts

System 7 offers lots of easy ways to customize the appearance of windows in the Finder. You can choose the font and font size for text displayed in windows, arrange icon views in a straight or staggered grid, calculate folder sizes and much more. All of these options are available through the Views control panel (don't confuse it with the View menu on the Finder). You'll find a complete discussion of this program in Chapter 8, p. 115.

Automatic scrolling

With System 6, when you wanted to move a document into a folder in the same window, and the window wasn't big enough to show both, you had to resize or scroll the window to bring both items into view.

Automatic scrolling ends this hassle. Now when you drag a document past the boundaries of a window, it automatically scrolls in the direction you're dragging.

Automatic scrolling only works within a window, not from one window to the next.

Other file management changes

Opening files

You can still open a file by doubleclicking its icon or choosing *Open* from the File menu. But System 7 also lets you open a document by dragging its icon on top of the icon for any program that can open it, not only the one you used to create it.

Here's an example. Let's say you want to view a Microsoft Works document with Microsoft Word. Instead of opening the Word program, and then the Works file from the File menu, you can simply drag the Works file on top of the icon for Microsoft Word in the Finder. Word will then load and automatically open the Works file.

This little trick only works when the application you want to use isn't currently running. (Obviously, if the program is already running, it's no extra step to open the document with the program's *Open* command.) If you drag a document to a program icon and the program can't open that type of document, you'll see a message telling you so.

As previously mentioned, you can also open documents or programs automatically when you start up your Mac by dragging them inside the Startup Items folder in the System Folder (see *Opening files automatically at startup*, Chapter 3, p. 38 or *The Startup Items folder* in Chapter 7, p. 98).

Copying and moving files

You still drag files to move them from one place to another in the Finder, but System 7 offers some new capabilities here as well, and it fixes a nagging problem.

In older system software versions, clicking an item you wanted to move would also activate the window containing it. And that sometimes covered up the folder you wanted to drag to. Look here, for example, at the following windows:

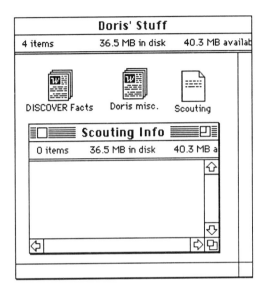

Under System 6 you couldn't drag the Scouting document from its present location into the Scouting Info folder, because the Doris' Stuff folder would become active as soon as you selected the document, and would cover up the Scouting Info folder.

But under System 7, if you hold down the mouse button when selecting a document, it won't activate the folder containing it, and so the destination folder is not covered up. This is a great example of how System 7 makes things work the way they always should have.

Finally, there's a new alert box that warns you when you're about to overwrite a file with the same name. Now, this alert tells you whether the file you're about to overwrite is older or newer than the one you're saving—a nice feature.

Deleting files

The Trash no longer empties itself automatically when you eject a disk, restart or shut down your Mac. You still see a warning when you drag any program or system software file to the Trash, which you can still disable by holding down [Option] as you select and drag the item. But now you'll also see a further warning when you try to empty the Trash:

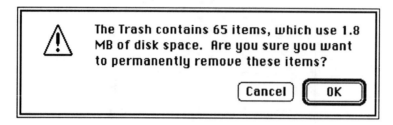

If this annoys you as much as it does me, you'll be relieved to know you can turn it off. See *The Empty Trash* command in Chapter 6, p. 83 for details.

FKeys

The combination of [Shift][⌘] and any of the number keys in the top row of the keyboard are designated in the system software as FKeys (Apple shorthand for function keys). Each combination performs the same function every time, no matter which program or window is active.

In this section, we'll focus on the four FKeys that have already been defined by Apple in System 7. Programs for other FKeys have been developed by hobbyist programmers and small software companies. You can find out about them from your local user group.

Ejecting floppy disks

Two of these FKeys work the same as they always have:

- [Shift][⌘][1] ejects the floppy disk in the internal drive (or the upper or left drive if you have two).

- [Shift][⌘][2] ejects the floppy disk in the external drive (or the lower or right drive if you have two).

Now, you can also eject a floppy disk from a third floppy drive (if you have one), by pressing ⟨Shift⟩ ⟨⌘⟩ ⟨O⟩.

(If you already have a floppy disk selected, you can press ⟨⌘⟩ ⟨E⟩ as usual, which is the same as choosing *Eject Disk* from the Special menu in the Finder.)

Taking screen snapshots

As before, the fourth FKey, ⟨Shift⟩ ⟨⌘⟩ ⟨3⟩, takes a snapshot of your Mac's screen and saves it as a file in the main directory of your startup disk. Now, though, your snapshot files are named *Picture 0*, *Picture 1*, and so on, numbered sequentially, rather than *Screen 0*, etc. More important, you can take as many snapshots as you want, provided you have the disk space—you no longer have to stop at *Screen 9*.

What's more, you can now open these files with the System 7 version of the TeachText program (on one of your utilities disks). Also, you can then select part or all of the image, copy it to the Clipboard, then paste it into the Scrapbook or into a document from another program.

(Snapshot files remain in PICT format, so you can still open them with lots of different paint or draw programs—you just don't have to.)

Keyboard shortcuts

You can use these keyboard shortcuts to do a lot of things you'd normally do with the mouse. You may be familiar with the old shortcuts, but the System 7 Finder has some really nice new ones.

The following descriptions are pretty brief—you really have to try these to appreciate how useful they are. (See *FKeys*, above, for other shortcuts.)

Selecting icons on the desktop

These shortcuts select icons that are directly on the desktop, such as disks, the Trash, or document or program icons you've put there. They don't work for selecting icons that are inside windows or for activating windows.

SHORTCUT KEY	ACTION
an arrow key	selects the next desktop icon in that direction
Tab	selects the next desktop icon in alphabetical order by name
a letter key	selects the first desktop icon whose name begins with that letter

Navigating folders or windows

When you've got your disk organized so folders are inside folders that are inside folders, you can use these shortcuts to navigate up and down the folder hierarchy (or directory path) or to open and close windows quickly. These select different folders in a window, or different nested windows on the desktop. (⌘↑ and ⌘↓ also work in the directory dialog box that you see when you use *Open* or *Save As* in a program.) Try them out for yourself.

4. WORKING WITH THE FINDER

SHORTCUT KEY(S)	ACTION
⌘ ↑	opens the folder that contains the current folder or selects it (if it's already open)
Option ⌘ ↑	opens the folder that contains the current folder and closes the current folder window
⌘ ↓	opens the selected icon or folder
Option doubleclick icon	opens the selected icon or folder and closes the current folder or window
Shift ⌘ ↑	selects the desktop itself (deselecting everything else)
⌘ →	shows outline view of selected folder's contents
⌘ ←	hides outline view of selected folder's contents
Option ⌘ →	shows outline view of active window
Option ⌘ ←	hides outline view of active window
Option click zoom box	expands a window to the maximum size it can be on the screen
Option drag icon	reverses the current setting of the *always snap to grid* checkbox in the Views control panel while moving the icon

Dialog box shortcuts

These three shortcuts help you deal with dialog boxes more quickly.

SHORTCUT KEY(S)	ACTION
Tab	moves the insertion point from one option to another in a dialog box
Return or Enter	clicks the heavily outlined button in a dialog box
⌘ .	clicks the *Cancel* button in a dialog box

File menu command shortcuts

These shortcuts let you select File menu commands by using the keyboard.

SHORTCUT KEYS	COMMAND
⌘ N	*New Folder*
⌘ O	*Open*
⌘ P	*Print*
⌘ W	*Close Window*
⌘ I	*Get Info*
⌘ D	*Duplicate*
⌘ Y	*Put Away*
⌘ F	*Find*
⌘ G	*Find Again*

Edit menu command shortcuts

Here are the shortcuts for the Edit menu commands.

SHORTCUT KEYS	COMMAND
⌘ Z	Undo
⌘ X	Cut
⌘ C	Copy
⌘ V	Paste
⌘ A	Select All

Special menu command shortcuts

Here are some shortcuts and special features of commands on the Special menu.

SHORTCUT KEY(S)	ACTION
Option Clean Up By Name	sorts the icons in an icon view window in alphabetical order, and aligns them in rows on an invisible grid—a window must be selected for this to work
Option Clean Up All	arranges all icons on the desktop except the Trash in a column in the upper right corner of the screen, puts the Trash in the lower right corner of the screen—the desktop itself (or an icon on it) must be selected for this to work
Option Empty Trash	stops the warning box from showing when you empty the Trash
⌘ E	ejects the selected floppy disk

Other shortcuts

Finally, these shortcuts help with other Finder activities.

SHORTCUT	ACTION
[Option] drag item	copies item instead of moving it
[Option] click close box (or [Option] [⌘] [W])	closes current window and all other windows on the desktop
[⌘] drag window by its title bar	moves window without making it active
[⌘] click a window title	shows the directory path of that window
[Shift] [Option] [⌘] while starting up	rebuilds the desktop file
hold down [Shift] while starting up	prevents any extension files (inits) from loading during startup

THE FINDER AND ITS MENUS

Chapter 5
File and Edit menu commands

THE FILE MENU **60**
    The Get Info command **61**
    The Sharing... command **66**
    The Make Alias command **66**
    The Find...
        and Find Again commands **70**
THE EDIT MENU **75**

The File menu has undergone significant changes in System 7, while the Edit menu looks exactly the same but may, in certain applications, contain new commands arising from System 7's new publish and subscribe feature.

THE FILE MENU

We'll look at these commands in the order in which they appear on the File menu.

Some commands are the same

The *New Folder, Open, Print* and *Close* commands work the same way, although the *Close* command is now called **Close Window** to more accurately describe what it does (anything you can close in the Finder is a window). The *Duplicate, Put Away, Page Setup* and *Print Window...* commands are the same, except that **Print Window...** used to be called *Print Directory....* Again, *Print Window* is a better way to say what this command actually does.

There are a couple of changes to the dialog box you see when you choose the *Print...* command, but we'll cover these in Chapter 10 along with other printing details.

Some commands have been moved or eliminated

Two File menu commands from System 6 are no longer on this menu. The *Get Privileges...* command is gone. If you're an AppleShare user, you can now view folder privileges with the new *Sharing...* command, which we'll get to on p. 66 of this chapter and in Chapter 11, p. 163.

You may notice that the *Eject* command is missing. It has been renamed **Eject Disk** and moved to the Special menu.

The Get Info command

The *Get Info* command displays information about any item whose icon you select in the Finder. A different information window will appear depending on whether you've selected a program, a document, an alias or a storage location (a folder or disk). The one new feature all these windows share is that you can change the icon of the item they describe.

Customizing icons

If you want to change an icon:

1. Select a graphic (or prepare your own using a paint or draw program) and copy it to the clipboard.

2. In the Finder, select the program, document, alias or volume whose icon you want to modify, and choose *Get Info*. The item's information window will be displayed.

3. Click on the icon in the information window. A box will appear around it. (If no box appears, then you can't change that particular item's icon.)

4. Choose *Paste* from the Edit menu. The new icon will replace the old one. (If it doesn't, make sure the *Locked* checkbox isn't checked and try again.)

Program information

When you select an application and choose *Get Info*, you'll see a window like this:

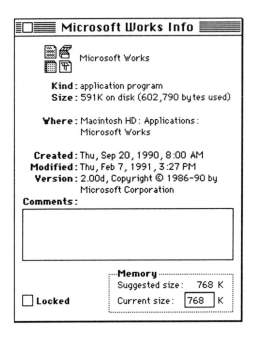

This window is for applications only, not for DAs, control panels or other system software, because applications let you adjust the requested memory and those other types of program don't.

The Version category right above the Comments box is the same as in System 6 (as before, when programs don't make their version information available to the system software, this area will say *not available*).

In the Memory section at the bottom, the names have changed from Suggested memory size and Application memory size to the simpler **Suggested size** and *Current size*. The suggested size is the amount of memory the application would normally ask for.

If you use big documents with an application, click its *Current size* box and enter a larger number. (It's best to up the ante by at least 20 percent, so if a program asks for 512K in the Suggested size box, try entering at least 640K in the *Current size* box.) Then close the window, and the new memory limit will be in effect the next time you open the program.

Don't give a program less memory than suggested. If you try, you'll see an alert message and the program probably won't run at all, or it will quit or crash unexpectedly later.

As with System 6, you can lock a program by checking the *Locked* checkbox (now relocated to the lower left corner of the window). Locking a program prevents it from being changed or erased, but it's not always a good idea, because some programs don't work properly when they're locked.

Document information

When you select a document and choose *Get Info*, you'll see a window that looks like this:

```
┌─────── Monthly Budget Info ───────┐
│  ┌──┐                              │
│  │📊│ Monthly Budget               │
│  └──┘                              │
│       Kind: Microsoft Works document│
│       Size: 3K on disk (3,062 bytes used)│
│                                    │
│      Where: Macintosh HD : Finances : Monthly│
│             Budget                 │
│                                    │
│    Created: Wed, Mar 7, 1990, 12:22 PM│
│   Modified: Thu, Dec 6, 1990, 9:00 AM│
│    Version: not available          │
│                                    │
│  Comments:                         │
│  ┌──────────────────────────────┐  │
│  │                              │  │
│  │                              │  │
│  └──────────────────────────────┘  │
│                                    │
│  ☐ Locked         ☐ Stationery pad │
└────────────────────────────────────┘
```

Like the window for applications, this one shows information about the file's location, kind, size, creation and modification dates and version. But notice the *Stationery pad* checkbox in the lower right corner (which is an option only for documents). It lets you turn a document into a stationery pad—a template which will always open as a new document.

For more information about this feature, see *Using stationery* in Chapter 9, p. 130.

Alias information

The information window that appears when you select an alias and choose *Get Info* is slightly different from the one for documents:

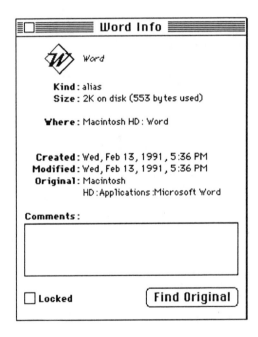

When you need to locate the file that an alias represents, click the **Find Original** button. The Mac will search for the original and then select it on the desktop (see *The Make Alias command* on p. 66 of this chapter for more information).

You can change aliases' icons or lock them using the information window. Changing an alias's icon doesn't affect the original file it represents. But note that *locking an alias really only protects its icon and title* (and prevents the alias itself from being deleted); you can modify or even delete an original while the alias is locked.

Folder or disk information

When you select a folder or a disk and use *Get Info*, you'll see a window like this:

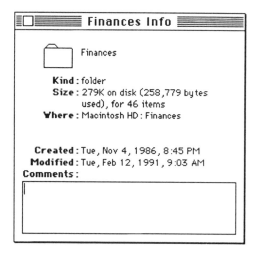

There's no box around the folder icon because it hasn't been selected yet, but you can still select it and replace it with another graphic, just as you can with documents.

Since this is a storage location rather than a file, there's no version information, and you don't have options to lock the folder or turn it into stationery.

The Sharing... command

The *Sharing...* command lets you make selected folders or even entire disks available to other Mac users on an AppleTalk network. You can also use it to view the access privileges for any shared disk or folder on the network.

File sharing gives you lots of options for sharing your files with others. Turn to Chapter 11 for a full discussion of this powerful new feature.

The Make Alias command

An alias is a stand-in file that allows you to open a real file, folder or disk by remote control. When you open an alias, it opens the real item that the alias represents.

This simple command can make it a lot easier to locate and open programs, documents, folders or disks on your Mac.

Making an alias

The procedure for making an alias is simple:

1. Select an item in the Finder or a Finder window.

2. Choose the *Make Alias* command from the File menu. An alias of the item immediately appears, overlapping it like this:

Notice that the alias's name is selected. When you first create it, an alias is always given the name in italics of the item you originally selected plus the word *alias*. You can, though, change the name to anything you want. The alias has the same icon as the item it represents.

There are two ways to tell an alias from a real item:

- An alias name always appears in italics on the desktop.
- An alias's Kind designation in a list view window or in the *Get Info* command's information window is always *alias*.

Using an alias

Once you create an alias, you can treat it like a normal file. You can:

- doubleclick it to open the item it represents
- copy items to it or open items inside it
- rename its icon just as you would any other icon (this doesn't rename the original file)
- duplicate, copy or move it to any other location on your Mac's desktop, such as another folder or another disk
- select it and use *Get Info* to display its information window
- drag it to the Trash when you don't need it anymore
- lock it to prevent it from being deleted and to prevent changes to its name or icon

Tips for using aliases

Because you can make several aliases for the same item and copy them anywhere, aliases make it much easier for you to find and open items you use a lot. And they take up very little disk space (usually only 1K or 2K).

System 7 comes with one alias already set up: the **Control Panels** alias inside the Apple Menu Items folder. The *real* Control Panels folder is inside the System Folder, but you can open it by choosing this alias from the menu. Below are some other ideas for using aliases.

Application aliases Most people store all their applications in the same folder. This makes organizational sense, but it means you have to open that folder every time you want to open a particular program. To avoid this problem, you can:

- make an alias of a program and put it on the desktop

- put aliases of programs you use every day in the Startup Items folder inside the System folder. Then they'll be opened each time you start up your Mac.

DA aliases DAs stored in the Apple Menu Items folder appear on the menu, so they're already pretty accessible, but since you can now open DAs by doubleclicking them, you can also make an alias of any DA you use a lot and put it on the desktop.

Control panel aliases If you use certain control panels frequently, put aliases of them in the Apple Menu Items folder so you can open them directly from the menu.

Folder aliases Try these ideas with folders you use a lot:

- Put a folder's alias in the Apple Menu Items folder, so you can open it from the menu. (You can even make an alias for the Apple Menu Items folder itself, so you can open it from the menu when you want to add or remove items.)

- Put an alias on the desktop so you can drag things into or out of the folder there, without having to open other folders to get to it.

- Put a folder's alias inside any other folder where you normally work. That way you can avoid navigating through folders in your programs' *Open* or *Save* dialog boxes when you're opening from or saving to that folder.

Shared folder aliases To connect to a shared folder over a network, you normally have to use the AppleShare resource in the Chooser and then enter your name and password. But if you make an alias of a shared folder or disk, you'll go directly to the user log-in dialog box when you open the alias; or—if no password or user name is required to connect to the shared item—the item will be automatically placed on your desktop. (See Chapter 11 for more information about connecting to shared folders and disks.)

Disk or Trash aliases You can even make aliases of hard disks or the Trash and put them in more convenient places—like the Apple Menu Items folder (so you can open them from the menu).

There are lots of uses for aliases, so explore a few of them for yourself. You can't hurt anything by creating an alias, and you can always get rid of any you don't want by dragging them to the Trash; your original file stays where it is.

Aliases that don't make sense

You can make an alias of any item on the desktop, but some aliases just don't serve any purpose. Since aliases are easy ways to open a file or access a folder, you don't need aliases for any files or folders you don't interact with. These include system software files like the Clipboard file in the System Folder, or special folders that some programs create automatically for their own use, like the PrintMonitor Documents folder.

Alias troubleshooting

If you try to open an alias and nothing happens, either the alias file is damaged or the original file has been deleted from the disk. To find out which is the culprit:

1. Select the alias and choose *Get Info*. The information window appears.

2. Click the *Find Original* button. Your Mac will attempt to find the original file.

If your Mac can't find the file, then the original has been deleted. Delete the alias, copy a new original file to your disk, and make a new alias.

If your Mac finds the file, the alias itself is damaged. Delete the alias and make a new one.

The Find... and Find Again commands

The *Find...* and *Find Again* commands let you locate files on any disk or shared folder available to your Mac. These commands replace the Find File DA that Apple included with previous versions of the system software.

The *Find...* command gives you a lot more flexibility than the old Find File did, and enables you to search through more than one disk or shared folder at a time. Once a file is found, *Find...* opens the folder containing it and selects it. This process was a lot clumsier with Find File.

The *Find Again* command lets you continue a search begun with *Find...*, so as to locate other files that match the same criteria.

Finding files by name

The *Find...* command offers two levels of file-finding options. Here's how the basic level works:

1. Choose *Find...* from the File menu. The Find dialog box appears:

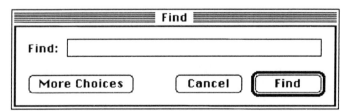

2. If you know all or part of the lost file's name, type it into the box. You can enter any contiguous part of a file's name to locate it—for example, the first few characters, a few characters in the middle of the name or the last few characters. Obviously,

the more complete the name, the more likely the Mac will find just the file you want, particularly if several files on the disk have similar names.

3. Click the *Find* button. The Mac automatically searches every disk or shared folder on your desktop alphabetically for the first name that matches what you typed in. (Depending on how many disks or shared folders and files there are, a search can take around fifteen seconds—but usually it takes less than five.)

If the Mac can't find a file that matches your search text, it will beep.

Finding files again using the same criterion

If more than one item's name contains your search text, the first one the Mac finds may not be the one you're looking for. To resume the search, use the *Find Again* command.

The *Find...* command stores the last search criterion you entered, so when you use the *Find Again* command you're asking the Mac for other files that match that criterion.

Here's an example. Suppose you have two files on your disk, one named Avenue and another named Venue. If you type *Venue* in the Find box, the Mac will find the file named Avenue first, because the letters you typed are part of that name, and Avenue comes before Venue in alphabetical order. (The Mac ignores upper and lower case text when it searches for files.) In this case, you'd have to use the *Find Again* command to search further for the Venue file.

If repeatedly searching for a file doesn't appeal to you, or if you want to see all the found files as a group, you'll need to use other Find options.

Finding files by size, kind or other criteria

To move to the second level of options available with the *Find...* command, choose *Find...* from the File menu, then click the *More Choices* button in the dialog box. An expanded Find dialog box appears, like this:

```
┌─────────────────────────────────────────────────┐
│═══════════════════════ Find ════════════════════│
│  Find and select items whose                     │
│  ┌─────────────▼┐  ┌─────────────▼┐ ┌──────────┐│
│  │    name      │  │   contains   │ │          ││
│  └──────────────┘  └──────────────┘ └──────────┘│
│  ..............................................│
│  Find within ┌──────────────▼┐    ☐ all at once │
│              │   all disks   │                   │
│              └───────────────┘                   │
│  ..............................................│
│  ┌──────────────┐            ┌────────┐ ┌──────┐│
│  │Fewer Choices │            │ Cancel │ │ Find ││
│  └──────────────┘            └────────┘ └──────┘│
└─────────────────────────────────────────────────┘
```

The default choices in this box offer exactly the same search capabilities as the basic Find dialog box. But when you click **name, contains** and **all disks,** pop-up menus appear, from which you choose to search for files by creation or modification date, kind, size, label, version, file comments or even by whether they're locked or not. (See *File-finding tips* relating to these options on p. 74 of this chapter.)

The pop-up menu for *contains* changes according to the choice you made with the *name* menu—as does the text box at the upper right. The type of information you enter here depends on the choices you made before on the pop-up menus; and in some cases, the text box itself becomes a pop-up menu of search options.

We could use up a lot of space here showing the various search criteria you can select, but you can see them all just as easily by exploring the menus yourself.

Once you've specified your search criteria in the pop-up menus and text box, just click the *Find* button or press Return or Enter. Try a few searches this way, and you'll soon get the idea.

The *Find...* command assumes you want to search every storage location available *(all disks* is the default choice), but you can use the **Find within** pop-up menu to restrict the search to just one of the storage locations on your desktop. In fact, you can restrict a search to just the active window in the Finder, or even to items that are currently selected (see the next section, *Searching selected items.*)

The *all at once* checkbox is handy when you want to find all the items on a disk or in a folder that match your search criteria. When you check this box the *Find within* menu automatically changes to show your startup disk, and the Mac will select and display all the found files in one list view window, like this:

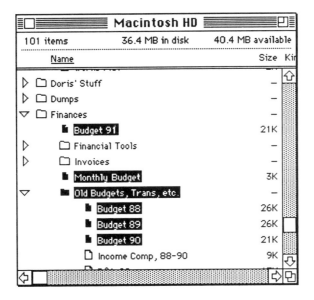

The actual window you see will probably be bigger than this example, and you'll probably still have to scroll it to see all the files that have been selected. But if all the items that match your search criterion are inside the same folder or otherwise close to each other in the list view structure, you'll be able to see them all at once.

Searching selected items

The one major limitation to your search options is that *the Mac can only use one search criterion at a time*. (In some third-party file-finding programs—CE Software's DiskTop, for example—you can search for a file with multiple criteria, specifying a file's date, kind, modification date or other information simultaneously.)

There *is* a partial work-around to this problem: once you've done an *all at once* search, you can then search among those found items with a different criterion. Here's how:

1. Choose the *Find…* command and click the *More Choices* button to display the expanded Find dialog box.

2. Specify the first search criterion and check the *all at once* checkbox.

3. Click the *Find* button. The Mac will find and select the files that match the criterion you specified.

4. Choose the *Find…* command again and click the *More Choices* button to display the expanded Find dialog box.

5. Specify the second search criterion.

6. Click on the pop-up menu next to *Find within*, and choose *the selected items* from this menu.

7. Click the *Find* button. The Mac will search among only the items selected in the first *Find* operation to locate ones that match your second criterion.

File-finding tips

In case it's not immediately obvious why you'd want to search for files by kind, label, modification date or some of the other criteria you can choose, here are a few suggestions:

Name is a good choice if you know a file's exact name, if you remember part of its name, or if you have several files with similar names and you want to find and select them all at once.

Kind is useful for finding all aliases, applications, documents, folders or stationery pad files. If you're backing up a disk, for example, you might want to select only documents to back up.

Size lets you find files above or below a certain size. If you use a lot of big graphics files, for example, you might want to locate them all so you can compress them or move them to another disk to free up space on your primary disk.

Label is only useful if you've actually *used* labels to identify certain files or folders on your disk. (See *The Label menu* Chapter 6, p. 77.) However, if you use labels to identify all the files belonging to a certain project, for example, you could find all those files at once and then back them up to the same disk.

Date created and *date modified* help you find recent files so you can back up those that have been created or changed since the last backup, or isolate older ones you may want to delete.

Comments will only help you find a specific file if you can remember the comments you made in its information window with the *Get Info* command. (You might have used a comment box, for example, to record some detailed notes about a file.)

Lock lets you find files that are locked. If you have locked files in a shared folder, for example, other users won't be able to change them. If you want to unlock such files quickly, search for them all at once.

THE EDIT MENU

The Edit menu and its commands look and work exactly the same under System 7 as under previous versions of the system software, as long as you're working in the Finder. You can undo the last thing you did; *Cut, Copy, Paste, Clear* or *Select All* the data in a document; or show the contents of the clipboard.

When you use the Edit menu from within an application, however, it may contain commands relating to System 7's new publish and subscribe feature. Publishing and subscribing are capabilities that must be supported by specific Mac applications. There are none at this writing, but you can expect lots of developers to support publish and subscribe soon. (For an overview of this feature, see *Publishing and subscribing,* Chapter 9, p. 133.)

THE FINDER AND ITS MENUS

Chapter 6
View, Label, Special, Help and Application menu commands

THE VIEW MENU **77**
THE LABEL MENU **77**
    Customizing labels **79**
THE SPECIAL MENU **81**
    The Clean Up commands **81**
    The Empty Trash command **83**
THE HELP MENU **84**
THE APPLICATION MENU **86**

This chapter covers changes to the Finder's View and Special menus and explains its new Label, Help and Application menus.

THE VIEW MENU

The View menu (don't confuse it with the Views control panel discussed in chapter 8) lets you choose the way items in Finder windows are displayed, as icons or as lists. As always, lists can be sorted by document names, dates, sizes or kinds.

Previously, users of color Macintosh systems used the Finder's Color menu to assign colors to window contents, and sorted them by color with the *by Color* command on the View menu. The System 7 Finder replaces the Color menu with the Label menu and lets you sort with the new *by Label* command on the View menu. As we'll see in the next section, labels provide much more flexibility in identifying and grouping desktop items, both by color and by label name.

THE LABEL MENU

The **Label menu** lets you assign one of seven label names to any item on the desktop, or to remove an existing label name from any item. If you have a color Mac and it's set to display at least sixteen colors or shades of gray, each name on the Label menu has a color or shade associated with it, and assigning a label to an item also gives the item that label's color or shade.

The standard Label menu on a black and white Macintosh looks something like this:

The labels shown above may be different in your version of System 7. In any case, you can use the Labels control panel to change the label names and colors (if you have a color Mac) to whatever you like. For information on doing this, see *Customizing labels* on the next page.

If you used the old Color command to assign colors to items on your disk under System 6, those items will automatically be given the label that corresponds to their color under System 7. Otherwise, none of the items on your disk will have labels when you first install System 7. (On the menu above, for example, the *None* command is checked because an unlabeled item was selected when this menu was displayed.) If items on your disk don't have labels, the Label column in a list view window of the Finder will look like this:

Labeling desktop items

Suppose you want to label the Invoice4/1 item in the window above as an *Essential* document. Simply select the item and then choose *Essential* from the Label menu. The invoice will take on the color that goes with the Essential label (if you have a color Mac) and the word *Essential* itself will appear in the Label column of the list view window, like this:

```
                   1990 Invoices
  Name                 Size  Kind              Label      Last Modi
  □ 1/15/90             2K   Microsoft Works d...  —     Sat, Ja
  □ 2/1/90              2K   Microsoft Works d...  —     Wed, J
  □ CWInvoice1/22/91    3K   Microsoft Word do...  —     Fri, Ja
  □ CWInvoice1/30/91    3K   Microsoft Word do...  —     Wed, J
  □ CWInvoice10/10      3K   Microsoft Word do...  —     Fri, Oc
  □ CWInvoice10/25      3K   Microsoft Word do...  —     Fri, Oc
  □ Invoice4/1          3K   Microsoft Word do... Essential  Tue, A
```

Sorting windows by label

If you use labels to identify items in Finder windows, you can sort the items by label names using the *by Label* command on the View menu. Items are sorted by their label's position on the Label menu (from top to bottom), rather than alphabetically by name. Unlabeled items follow labeled ones.

Try applying some labels yourself and then using the *by Label* command on the View menu to sort labeled items.

Customizing labels

If you use labels a lot, you'll probably want to change their names to more accurately reflect your organizational scheme or priority levels. You can change the names on the Label menu at any time with the Labels control panel.

1. Choose *Control Panels* from the menu.

2. Open the Labels icon. You'll see a control panel like this:

Again, the label names may be different on your Mac. Also, if you have a color monitor set to display sixteen or more colors, those boxes to the left of the labels will appear in the colors assigned to those labels.

Changing a label name

1. Doubleclick on the label name to select it.

2. Type a new name or edit the current one.

3. Press [Return] or [Enter] to confirm the change, or press [Tab] to confirm the change and move to the next label in the list.

Label name changes take effect as soon as you confirm them—not just on the Label menu, but everywhere the old label was used.

Changing a label color

Click on the color you want to change. The standard Macintosh color picker dialog box appears. Follow the instructions in Chapter 8 to select a new color.

THE SPECIAL MENU

The Finder's Special menu lets you organize the contents of windows, empty the Trash, erase or eject disks and restart or shut down the Mac.

The *Restart, Shut Down* and *Erase Disk...* commands work the same way they always have. The *Eject Disk* command (called simply *Eject* in earlier system versions) has moved to the Special menu from its old location on the File menu.

The old *Set Startup...* command that used to be on the Special menu is gone, its functions now handled with the Startup Items folder (see Chapter 7, p. 98).

The Clean Up commands

The *Clean Up* command arranges icons in windows or on the desktop in a regular pattern. As before, there are actually four different commands depending on what you have selected and whether or not you're holding down (Option). The command names are now more descriptive.

Clean Up commands work only on icon view windows or on the Finder desktop itself, not on list view windows.

The invisible grid

There's an invisible grid that underlies icon view windows and the desktop itself (you actually have a choice of two grids—see the Views control panel description in Chapter 8, p. 115). When you clean up items, you're telling the Finder to move them to points on the invisible grid. The grid has been around since before System 6, but the *Clean Up* command in System 7 uses it a little more intelligently.

If you select one icon and clean it up, only that icon moves. Select a window or the desktop and clean it up, and all its items move to grid points.

Cleaning up the desktop

Here are the *Clean Up* commands you get with the desktop selected. To select the desktop, select any icon on it, or click in the background area so nothing is selected. Once you've done this:

- The command becomes **Clean Up Desktop** and choosing it moves each item on the desktop to its nearest grid point.

- If you hold down (Option), the command becomes **Clean Up All** and choosing it moves every desktop icon except the Trash into a column in the upper right corner of the desktop. The Trash icon is moved to the lower right corner of the desktop if it isn't there already.

Cleaning up windows

To use the *Clean Up* commands in windows, select an icon view window or an icon inside a window.

- With a window selected, the command becomes **Clean Up Window**, and choosing it moves every icon in the window to its nearest grid point.

- With an icon inside a window selected, the command becomes **Clean Up Selection**, and choosing it moves that icon to its nearest grid point.

- If you hold down (Option) with a window or an icon in a window selected, the command becomes **Clean Up By Name**, and it arranges all the icons in the window into rows and columns along the invisible grid and puts them in alphabetical order by name.

The Empty Trash command

This command looks the same as before but it works a little differently because the Trash itself works differently in System 7.

Before System 7, the Trash was automatically emptied whenever you shut down or restarted the Mac, when you ejected a disk containing a file you'd dragged to the Trash, and usually when applications started up or quit. Under System 7, items you throw in the Trash stay there until you tell the Mac to empty the Trash. This gives you better protection against accidentally throwing things away.

Furthermore, System 7 doesn't just warn you as you drag your programs or system files to the Trash. It also gives you a message when you try to empty it, like this:

You must then click the *OK* button to empty the Trash.

Turning the Trash warning off

If you're not crazy about having to deal with this dialog box every time you delete a file, you can turn it off.

To do this only once, hold down (Option) when you choose the *Empty Trash* command. To turn it off indefinitely:

1. Select the Trash icon.

2. Choose *Get Info* from the File menu. The Trash information window appears, like this:

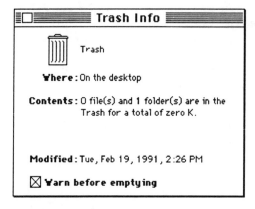

3. Uncheck the *Warn before emptying* checkbox.

4. Close the window.

Now you won't ever see the warning when you choose the *Empty Trash* command. If you decide you want the warning back, just repeat steps 1–4 above, checking the warning box in step 3.

THE HELP MENU

The **Help menu** is new in System 7. It lets you turn System 7's new built-in help balloons on and off, and it also lets you display a list of keyboard shortcuts for your Mac. Like the menu and the Application menu, the Help menu is available at all times, whether you're using the Finder or another application.

Balloon Help

Balloon Help is a built-in feature of System 7 that displays pop-up balloons describing various items on the screen as you point to them.

Balloon Help works automatically once you turn it on by selecting *Show Balloons* from the Help menu. It describes things like windows, documents, buttons, checkboxes, menus and menu commands. Here's an example:

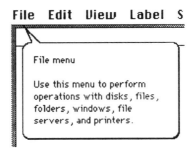

In this case, the pointer is on the File menu, so the balloon explains what the File menu does. Along with Finder icons, windows, menus and commands, the Balloon Help that comes with System 7 also explains:

- each file and folder in the System Folder
- each DA on the menu
- each control panel in the Control Panels folder
- any document or disk on the desktop or in a window

Balloon Help is at present only available for the Mac's own system software, but other software publishers will eventually use it to provide information about their programs.

As a result, Apple-supplied files have better Balloon Help descriptions than non-Apple files. For example, if you point to the Keyboard icon in the Control Panels folder, you get a description of what the Keyboard control panel is used for. If you point to a non-Apple control panel icon, on the other hand, the balloon just says it's a control panel and that you can use it to customize part of your system.

Balloon Help is useful if you don't recognize an item in a window or you don't know what a button or command is for. But having all those balloons popping up can be really distracting once you know what you're doing. Even when you're working in an application, pointing to some common Mac features such as the , Help or Application menus or a window's title bar will cause balloons to pop up.

Fortunately, it's easy to turn Balloon Help on or off as you need it. Once you choose the *Show Balloons* command, the command name changes to *Hide Balloons*. Choose that command to turn Balloon Help off.

The *About Balloon Help...* command simply displays a dialog box that explains how to use the Balloon Help function. Try it and see.

Finder Shortcuts

The *Finder Shortcuts* command displays a dialog box listing several keyboard shortcuts. (For a complete list of System 7 keyboard shortcuts, see the *Keyboard Shortcuts* section at the end of Chapter 4.) As with Balloon Help, this command will be the gateway to lists of keyboard shortcuts for non-Apple applications as developers come to support it.

THE APPLICATION MENU

The **Application menu**, indicated by an icon at the far right of the menu bar, is the last new menu in the System 7 Finder. You use it to activate different programs you have running or to hide the windows of programs you aren't currently using so things are easier to see on the desktop.

This menu is always available in the menu bar, but the icon identifying it changes to the icon of whatever program's currently active on your Mac—a small Mac icon, say, if you're in the Finder, or the compass and paintbrush icon if you're in SuperPaint.

The bottom half of the menu lists all the programs you have running, so that also changes as you use your Mac. Click on the icon and the menu will appear, like this:

This particular menu indicates that the Finder, Microsoft Word and SuperPaint are all currently running on this Mac. The check mark next to Microsoft Word shows that it's the active application. We also know this from the Word icon that identifies the menu in the menu bar.

Activating a program

To activate a different program on the menu, just select it. (You can also click in a program's window on the desktop to activate it.)

To add another program to the menu, just start the program up. Once it's running, its name is added to the Application menu. When you quit a program, its name is automatically removed from the menu.

Remember, you can tell which program is currently active because:

- its window is active in the Finder
- its menus show in the menu bar
- its icon shows at the right end of the menu bar
- its name is checked on the Application menu

Hiding and showing windows

The *Hide* command changes to show the name of whichever program is currently active. In the example above, Microsoft Word is the active program, so this command says *Hide Microsoft Word*. When you choose this command, Microsoft Word's menus and any document windows it has open will be hidden from view, and the program's name is dimmed on the Application menu.

To reveal a program's windows after you've hidden them, just choose the program's name from the bottom part of the Application menu. Even though the name is dimmed, choosing it still activates the program and displays its windows.

The *Hide Others* command hides the windows of every program *except* the one that's currently active. On the Application menu shown above, for example, choosing *Hide Others* would hide any SuperPaint windows and any disk or folder windows open in the Finder. You can't hide the Finder desktop itself, because it isn't a window.

The *Hide Others* command is helpful when you have lots of Finder or program windows open and it's hard to maneuver around them to see the particular window you're working with.

The *Show All* command simply opens up all the windows you'd previously hidden with the *Hide* or *Hide Others* commands.

THE NEW SYSTEM FOLDER

Chapter 7
The System Folder

The System Folder **90**

The Apple Menu Items folder **91**

The Control Panels folder **95**

The Extensions folder **96**

The Preferences folder **97**

The PrintMonitor Documents folder **97**

The Startup Items folder **98**

The System file:
  installing fonts and sounds **99**

The System Folder has always been the Mac's nerve center. But in System 7 it does a lot more than store vital files, and the System file itself handles fonts and sounds differently. In this chapter you'll see how to use both the System Folder and the System file to customize and control your Mac. Chapter 8 covers control panels, which have their own folder within the System Folder.

The System Folder

When you first open the System Folder after installing System 7, you'll see an icon view window like this:

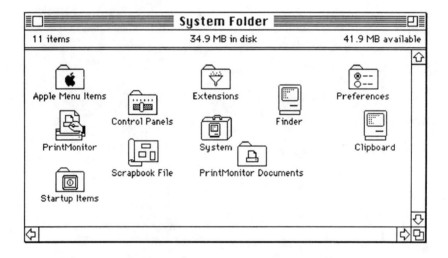

Although some icons look different, the new System Folder contains familiar items like the Finder, System, Clipboard, Scrapbook File and PrintMonitor. The folders, which are all new, are designed to store specific types of files used by the system software.

Installing files in the System Folder

The System Folder in System 7 is intelligent. Once you've started up your Mac with it, you can install most other system software files (like your own DAs, fonts or init files) simply by dragging them on top of the System Folder icon.

When you do this, the System Folder checks the file type of the item you're dragging. If it recognizes that type as belonging in a certain folder, it asks if you want to go ahead and put it there, like this:

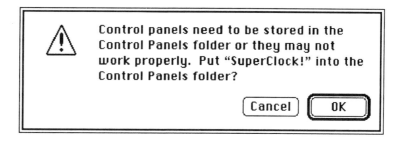

If the System Folder doesn't recognize a file type, the item will just be put inside the System Folder itself. These files may still work normally even though they're not inside the proper folder. On the other hand, some of your old System Folder files won't work under System 7 even if you do put them in the proper folders.

Now let's look at each of these folders.

The Apple Menu Items folder

In System 7, the menu has become a place where you can put anything you want to be able to find and open quickly, whether it's a document, folder, program, DA or other item. Anything you put in the Apple Menu Items folder will appear on the menu. There's no absolute limit—it used to be 15—on the number of items you can put on the menu, except the amount of space on your disk.

In a standard System Folder, the Apple Menu Items folder looks like this:

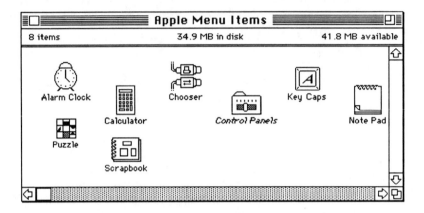

(If you have a Mac Portable, your folder may have a couple of extra DAs in it for monitoring battery use or setting the screen brightness.) Because these items are in the Apple Menu Items folder, their names show up on the ✜ menu like this:

Choosing a name from the ✜ menu opens the corresponding item from inside the Apple Menu Items folder. This procedure works for desk accessories, programs, documents or folders, as well as aliases. (For more about aliases, see *Aliases on the menu* on p. 94, or *The Make Alias command* in Chapter 5, p. 66.)

Installing desk accessories

Most of the items on System 7's standard menu are desk accessories (DAs). The DAs that come with System 7 are individual programs with unique icons that you can doubleclick to open, just like other applications. (You could even store these DAs in some completely different folder, and open them by doubleclicking there.)

DAs that came out before System 7 are stored in suitcase files like this:

A suitcase file can store one or more DAs. To install all the DAs from a suitcase file, just drag the suitcase icon directly on top of the System Folder icon. When you do this, the System Folder recognizes the suitcase file, opens it and installs the DA(s) in the Apple Menu Items folder. You don't need a special utility to do this, like System 6's Font/DA Mover.

If you're dragging a suitcase file to the System Folder icon from somewhere else on your startup hard disk, the Mac will try to delete the empty suitcase file after copying its DA(s) into the Apple Menu Items folder. Sometimes this doesn't work and you'll see a message saying it didn't (in that case, delete the empty suitcase file yourself).

If you want to manually remove a DA from its suitcase file (which you need to do if you don't want to install all the DAs in a suitcase), here's the procedure:

1. Doubleclick on the suitcase icon. You'll see a window like this:

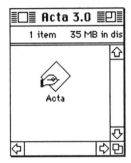

(You can tell this is an older DA, because it has a generic application icon rather than a unique one.)

2. Drag the DA(s) you want out of this window (and into the Apple Menu Items folder if you want to install them on the menu).

Installing documents, folders or programs on the menu

If you want to install a program, document or folder on the menu, just drag the item into the Apple Menu Items folder. When you want to put an item on the menu but you don't want to store it in the Apple Menu Items folder, use an alias.

Aliases on the menu

If you have anything that you open frequently and it's buried deep inside other folders, you can easily make an alias for it and put it in the Apple Menu Items folder. Then choosing the alias name from the menu will open that item. (For more on making aliases, see *The Make Alias command* in Chapter 5, p. 66.)

The Control Panels folder you see in the Apple Menu Items folder isn't the real one—it's an alias for it. Alias file names always appear in *italics* in Finder windows, and generally end with the word *alias* when they appear on the menu (except in this one instance, System 7's only built-in alias). Apple puts an alias for the Control Panels folder in the Apple Menu Items folder so it can keep the real Control Panels folder directly in the System Folder, where it's easier to find. (See *The Control Panels folder* below for more information.)

menu items you don't want

Theoretically, you can put anything you want in the Apple Menu Items folder, but it doesn't make sense to put nonopenable files like the Clipboard or preferences files in it.

The System file has to remain directly inside the System Folder (not in some other folder within the System Folder) so putting it inside the Apple Menu Items folder will cause big problems. If you want to be able to open it from the menu (to add fonts, say), put an alias of the System file in the Apple Menu Items folder.

The Control Panels folder

As with DAs, you can now open control panel programs like applications; when you doubleclick one, it displays the options you have available. You can store them anywhere you want on a disk. The Control Panels folder is just a convenient place, because it lets you quickly display and access them using the *Control Panels* alias on the menu.

Once you open the Control Panels folder, you'll see familiar programs like Mouse, Keyboard and Color, along with some new ones that give you even more control over the look and feel of your Mac. For more information about all the control panels that come with System 7, see Chapter 8.

Most control panels become active as soon as you copy them to your disk and open them, but some, like screen-saver and clock programs, don't start working until you restart your Mac.

The Extensions folder

The **Extensions** folder stores init files and Chooser resources such as printer, scanner or network drivers. Under System 7, these files are all called **system extensions**. (You can see this by looking at the Kind category for, say, a printer driver in a text view window.)

Any system extension file will automatically be placed inside the Extensions folder when you drag its icon on top of the System Folder icon in the Finder (or you can drag extension files into the Extensions folder yourself).

In most cases, extension files will also work if they're located directly inside the System Folder, and not in the Extensions folder. But the Extensions folder lets you organize them all in one place and still have them work properly. If you put extension files inside any folder other than the Extensions folder or the System Folder, they probably won't work.

Chooser resources such as networking, scanner and printer drivers, are extensions that will work as soon as you copy them into the Extensions folder.

Init files include items like the Apple CD-ROM init (which makes your Mac recognize a CD-ROM player as a storage device), Capture (a screen dump utility) and QuickMail (the init that starts up the QuickMail electronic mail program). These extensions are activated only when the Mac starts up, so if you drag an init file into the Extensions folder, you'll have to restart the Mac before it will begin working.

The Preferences folder

This folder stores settings you've chosen for specific operations like sharing files with users or groups, viewing documents in the Finder and displaying system extension files like clocks or other enhancements. A lot of applications like PageMaker, Microsoft Word or Excel create their own preferences files.

Applications that know about the Preferences folder will store their preferences files there, and others will store them directly in the System Folder. You should leave a preferences file wherever it happens to be so that the program that created it will be able to find it. As developers come to support System 7, you can expect newer versions of applications to store their preference files inside the Preferences folder.

The PrintMonitor Documents folder

This folder is automatically created by the PrintMonitor program when you first print a document with background printing turned on. As seasoned MultiFinder and LaserWriter users know, PrintMonitor is the printer spooler that comes with Macintosh system software. (See *Using PrintMonitor*, Chapter 10, p. 147 for more information.)

When PrintMonitor starts up, it looks for a PrintMonitor Documents folder in the System Folder. If there is no such folder, PrintMonitor will create one. PrintMonitor quickly "prints" your document into that folder, and then feeds the document to your printer at a slower pace while you get on with other work.

Unless PrintMonitor is in the process of sending a file to your printer, the PrintMonitor Documents folder is empty. Don't bother deleting this folder, though; PrintMonitor will only create a new one the next time you print a document.

The Startup Items folder

This **Startup Items** folder replaces the old *Set Startup...* command on the Special menu in the Finder. It stores documents, DAs or programs you want to open automatically whenever you start up your Mac. To have a program or document open automatically, just drag it (or an alias for it) inside this folder. The next time you start up, that document or program will be opened.

If you drag a document into the folder, your Mac will automatically find and load the program that created it, provided that program is on your hard disk. If the program can't be found, you'll see a message that says so.

Every program you open uses up memory. If you drag more programs into the Startup Items folder than your Mac can hold in its memory, not all of them will open. The Mac will open as many programs as it can, and then you'll see a message that there isn't enough memory to open the others.

To turn a startup item back into an ordinary document or program, you must drag it completely out of the System Folder, not just out of the Startup Items folder.

Startup items that don't belong here

Although some people refer to inits as "startup files," the Startup Items folder isn't where they belong. As explained on p. 96 of this chapter, init files are system extensions and should be stored in the Extensions folder.

Also, don't copy a folder into the Startup Items folder. If you do, the Mac will try to open everything inside that folder. If you want a folder to be open on your desktop each time you start your Mac, just leave it open when you shut down.

The System file: installing fonts and sounds

In System 7, fonts and sounds are still installed in the System file, but you no longer need a special utility to install them. You can open the System file itself and doubleclick on any font to display it, or on any sound to play it. Simply drag fonts or sounds into or out of the System file's window to install or remove them.

All this sounds really nice and straightforward, but nothing is ever as simple as it seems. Let's take a closer look.

Opening the System file

You can view the contents of the System file at any time by doubleclicking on the System file icon. When you do, you'll see a window like this:

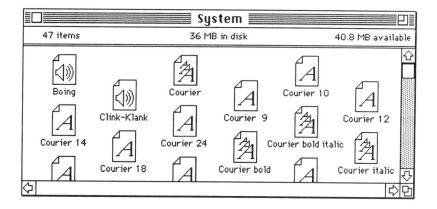

This particular window shows sound files (Boing and Clink-Clank), fixed-size font files (Courier 14, for example) and TrueType font files (Courier, Courier bold and Courier italic).

Playing sounds and viewing fonts

Once the window is open, you can play any sound by doubleclicking on it. Doubleclicking a fixed-size font file displays a sample of the font in that size, like this:

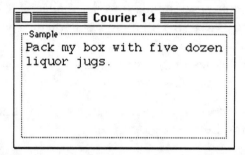

TrueType is Apple's new scalable font technology. With it, you use the same font to display type on the screen as you do to print out a file, and you can make a font just about any size and still keep its nice, smooth appearance on the screen and on paper. If you doubleclick a TrueType font you'll see samples of the font in three different sizes, like this:

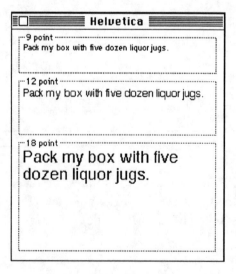

For more about TrueType, see Chapter 10.

Font and sound file formats

Before System 7, font files were stored in suitcase files (similar to DA suitcase files), like this:

All Fonts

A suitcase file could contain one or several fonts. You used the Font/DA Mover to open suitcase files and install specific fonts in the System file, or you could use a font management utility like Suitcase to open font files and make them available to the System file.

With System 7, you can open suitcase files by doubleclicking on them, and you can install font files by dragging them onto the System file's icon (see *Installing fonts and sounds* on the following page).

Sounds on the Mac have always been handled with shareware utilities, like Sound Manager or Sound Mover, in previous versions of the system software. If your sounds are stored in a separate file (outside the System file), you should still be able to use these utilities to install sounds. Just make sure the sound files are *snd* resources. (Most shareware sound management programs either create snd resources or can convert sound files into snd resources.) If they are, and they're also individual files, you can install them by dragging them into the System file window, as explained below. If your sound files aren't snd resources, you'll have to convert them with your sound installation utility before you'll be able to install them.

Changing the System file

You can't make any changes to the System file while anything but the Finder is running. If you try, you'll see a message warning that you have to close any other applications first.

So after making System file changes, you'll have to restart any programs you had closed. But you don't have to restart the Mac. Any changes you make to the System file take effect immediately.

Installing fonts or sounds

Assuming you've quit all your programs except the Finder, you're ready to install fonts or sounds. There are three ways to do it:

- Drag a font file, font suitcase or sound file on top of the System Folder icon. You'll see a message asking if you want to install the font or sound in the System file. Click the *OK* button to do so.

- Drag the font file, font suitcase or sound file on top of the System file icon. The file(s) will be installed.

- Doubleclick the System file to open its window, then drag a font or sound file inside it. You can't drag a font suitcase into the System file; you must open the suitcase file yourself and drag the font(s) from the suitcase file's window to the System file window. If you've stored a lot of fonts in one big suitcase and don't want to install them all, this approach lets you select the fonts you want.

THE NEW SYSTEM FOLDER

Chapter 8
Using control panels

The Control Panels folder **104**

Some control panels are the same **106**

Familiar control panels
  with new features **106**

The Views control panel **115**

Other new control panels **119**

Control panels are individual programs that let you set user preferences for the Finder or elsewhere in the system software's operations. (In System 6, they were called control panel devices, or cdevs.) In this chapter, we'll look at the standard control panels that come with System 7. As you'll see, many of them work much as they did before; others may have familiar names but operate differently; some are totally new.

The Control Panels folder

In previous versions of the system software, the Control Panel was a DA on the menu, with a scrolling list of cdevs in its dialog box. Under System 7, control panels are separate programs, and they're inside the **Control Panels folder** in the System Folder. (You can still access them from the menu, though, because choosing *Control Panels* there opens the folder for you.) Control panels can now be opened just like applications, and they can display more options than in the old dialog box—as many as will fit on the screen. The collection of programs in System's 7 Control Panels folder looks like this:

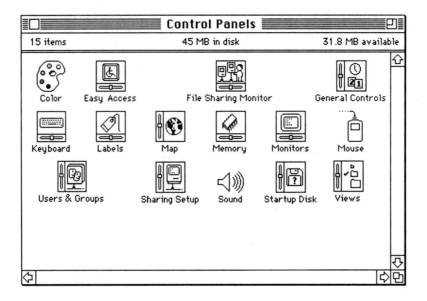

To use any of these, doubleclick its icon. The control panel will open and you'll see some options. For example, doubleclicking on the Startup Disk icon shows this control panel (as mentioned in the Introduction, *control panel* is Apple's name for a control panel's window):

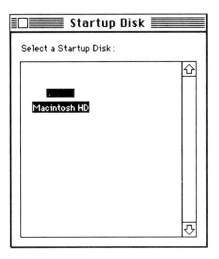

This control panel shows all the disks (just one in this case) currently connected to your Mac. This control panel differs from the old Startup Device cdev only in the way it's opened.

Making control panels easier to use

For even quicker access to a particular control panel, put an alias for it on the menu so you won't have to mess with the Control Panels folder at all.

For more about using aliases, see *The Make Alias command* in Chapter 5, p. 66.

Some control panels are the same

Of the fifteen control panels that come with the System 7, four are unchanged: Map, Monitors, Mouse and Startup Disk. (Startup Disk used to be called Startup Device, but it's otherwise the same.)

The only other change you'll see in these four programs is the pointer. Before System 7, you used a crosshair pointer to select a control panel's options. Now the pointer is the same kind of arrow you see in the Finder.

Another control panel that hasn't changed, but doesn't automatically get installed in the Control Panels folder, is CloseView. CloseView magnifies the Mac's screen for people with impaired vision. It comes on one of the System 7 Utilities disks, but if you want to use it all the time, drag it inside the Control Panels folder so you can get to it more easily.

Familiar control panels with new features

The other control panels whose names you'll recognize from previous system versions have some significantly different features in System 7. We'll look at those in detail here.

Color

The Color control panel has been expanded in System 7. Before, you could only adjust the color used to highlight selected text. Now, you can change the color of window borders as well. When you doubleclick the Color control panel, you'll see this window:

The **Highlight color** and **Window color** pop-up menus list the colors you can select (with the actual color displayed next to each one if your Mac can do this). The Window color menu has nine standard colors on it that can't be changed.

Clicking on the Highlight color menu makes its color selections appear like this:

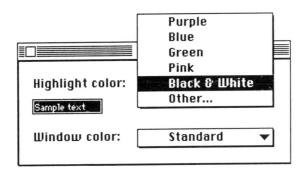

The *Other...* command shown here lets you choose any one of over 16 million colors with the standard Macintosh color picker. To select any one of them:

1. Choose the *Other...* command on the menu. The color picker dialog box appears, like this:

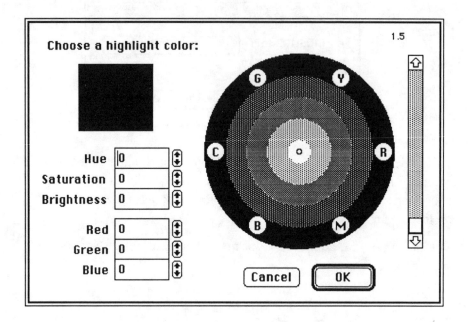

(This example was taken from a Mac set to display in black and white. That's why the color values in the lower left corner all read zero.)

The wheel in the color picker shows a range of colors that includes the highlight color currently being used (you'll see it in the box at the upper left). The G, Y, R, M, B and C on the wheel stand for green, yellow, red, magenta, blue and cyan, respectively.

2. Point to a place on the color wheel and click. That color will appear in the top left-hand box. Holding down the mouse button and dragging the pointer around the wheel will change the current color.

Because the Mac can produce over 16 million colors and you can't see them all in the color wheel at one time, you can use the scroll bar to show others. If you want to choose a color by its numeric color component values, click the arrows next to the Hue, Saturation, Brightness, Red, Green or Blue boxes to select the values you want.

3. When the color you want is shown in the current color box, click the *OK* button. The change will take effect immediately.

Easy Access

The **Easy Access** control panel makes the Mac easier to use for people who have trouble using the mouse or keyboard normally, or who want to choose multiple-key commands with just one hand.

Before System 7, Easy Access was an init program that had no user-adjustable features. Now the program is a control panel, and you can set several new options for it. When you open it, you see this:

The Mouse Keys and Sticky Keys features shown here are basically the same as in the old version of Easy Access, except now you can modify the way they work, not just turn them on or off. Slow Keys is new with System 7. Taking them from the top:

The *Use On/Off audio feedback* checkbox lets you tell the Mac to make a little siren sound whenever you turn one of Easy Access's three features on or off. Uncheck the box to shut the siren off.

The *On* and *Off* buttons for each of the following features turn it on and off (but you knew that).

Mouse Keys lets you control the pointer on the screen and perform other mouse activities by pressing numbers on your numeric keypad, like this:

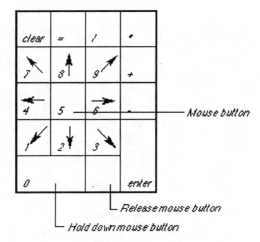

Clicking one of the directional number keys moves the mouse incrementally; holding one down sets it in continuous motion in that direction. You can see that the direction keys all form a circle around the 5 key. The 5 key itself works like the mouse button: press it once or twice to click or doubleclick the mouse button.

Since Mouse Keys users sometimes have trouble pressing more than one key at a time, other keys can be used to help select and drag an item on the screen. Press ⓞ (zero) and it'll hold the mouse button down while you drag an item with one of the directional keys. Press ⏺ to release the mouse button if you've been holding it down with the ⓞ key.

Note that you can't type numbers using the numeric keypad when Mouse Keys is on.

The *Initial Delay* buttons let you decide how long the Mac waits between the time you begin holding down a keypad key and the time it puts the pointer in continuous motion. The *Maximum Speed* buttons let you control the fastest rate at which the pointer moves across the screen. (The longer you hold down a key, the faster the pointer moves, but the maximum speed buttons let you determine the pointer's top speed.)

Slow Keys helps people who have trouble pressing keys or taking their fingers off of them quickly. It turns off the Mac's key repeat feature, so a string of characters doesn't print across the screen.

The *Acceptance Delay* buttons let you set the length of time you must hold down a key for that keystroke to take effect. The *Use key click sound* checkbox lets you add an audible click, which you'll hear after each character appears on the screen. Uncheck the box to get rid of the clicking sound.

Sticky Keys lets you type two-key commands without having to press both keys at the same time. Normally, to issue a keyboard command, you have to hold down a modifier key (Shift , ⌘ , Option or Ctrl) at the same time as you press another key. Sticky Keys lets you press the two (or more) keys in sequence.

When you turn Sticky Keys on, the Sticky Keys icon appears to the right of the Application menu in the menu bar, like this:

Then you can press a modifier key. An arrow appears above the Sticky Keys icon, indicating the modifier key has been set. Press the second key in the command to finish the command.

Normally, the modifier key will be released when the command is finished. If you want to use the same modifier key for a series of commands, you can lock it down by pressing it twice. The Sticky Keys icon darkens to indicate that a modifier key is locked down.

You can also "hold down" two of the four modifier keys at the same time by pressing them one after the other. For example, if you wanted to type [Shift][⌘][B], you'd press [Shift], then [⌘], and finally [B]. Both the [Shift] and [⌘] keys would be "held down" in this case.

To turn Sticky Keys off, either click the *Off* button in the control panel or press two modifier keys at the same time.

The ***Beep when modifier key is set*** checkbox lets you turn on a beep to notify you when a modifier key is set. This way, you don't always have to watch the Sticky Keys icon—you can just listen for the beep.

General Controls

The **General Controls** control panel replaces the General cdev in older versions of the Mac's system software. It's the same except the RAM cache options that used to be at the bottom of the box have been transferred to the Disk Cache area of the new Memory control panel (see *Memory*, p. 120).

Keyboard

The Keyboard control panel has the same Key Repeat Rate and Delay Until Repeat controls it's had for years, but now you can also use it to assign different international character sets to your keyboard. In the **Keyboard Layout** list, you'll see the names of keyboard character sets currently installed in your System file, like this:

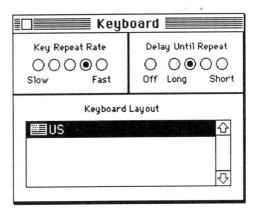

The only one supplied in the American version of System 7 is the US set shown above. In some other countries, you may be able to choose from two or more. Others are available through your Apple dealer.

As with fonts and sounds, you install additional keyboard character sets in the System file: doubleclick the System file to open it, drag your new keyboard file inside the System file's window and close the window. The new keyboard file will then appear in the Keyboard control panel's list and you can select it there.

Sound

Some of the latest Mac models (the LC and the IIsi) come with microphones for recording sounds. (Even if you have an older Mac, you can get MacRecorder from Farallon Computing, Inc., in Emeryville, California which will also let you edit what you record.) Once you've recorded your sounds, you can use them as Alert sounds instead of the beep your Mac usually makes.

The Sound control panel was changed in later versions of System 6, but since many Mac owners may not have used its new features, we'll look at them here. When you open the Sound control panel, it looks like this:

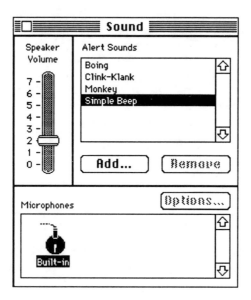

The sliding Speaker Volume control in this box is the same as ever. In the list of currently installed Alert Sounds, you can click on any sound's name to select it to play. If you select any sound except the Simple Beep, the *Remove* button becomes active, and you can use it to remove a sound from the list, which deletes it from the System file as well. You can't remove the Simple Beep (that's why clicking on it doesn't activate the *Remove* button).

The Microphones list at the bottom shows microphones currently connected to your Mac, and lets you switch between them for recording. Just click on the microphone you want to select it.

The *Options...* button is only active when you're using Farallon's MacRecorder driver or another enhanced sound input driver. Clicking this button lets you select which port the microphone is connected to.

The *Add...* button lets you record a new sound. When you click this button, you'll see a dialog box that lets you record or play sounds, like this:

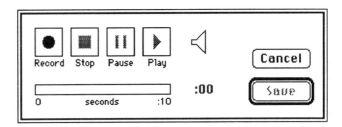

Click the *Record* button to begin recording. You'll see little sound wave lines coming out of the speaker icon, and a black line will begin filling the seconds bar to show you how much time you've spent recording. There's also a counter to the right of the seconds bar. The *Stop*, *Pause* and *Play* buttons all work just as they would on an ordinary tape recorder.

When you're done recording a sound, click the *Stop* button. The *Save* button will then become active. Click the *Save* button and you'll see a standard directory dialog box you can use to name and save the sound. Once you've done that, you can install it in your System file by dragging it on top of the System icon in the System Folder. After you've installed the sound, it will appear in the Alert Sounds list.

The Views control panel

The new **Views** control panel lets you customize Finder windows. You can change the default layout of icons in icon view windows, change the font or size of text used in Finder windows or on the desktop, and control the amount of information displayed about each item in a list view window. Let's have a look.

Choose *Control Panels* from the menu. The Control Panels folder opens on the desktop. Doubleclick on the Views icon in the folder. The Views control panel will open, like this:

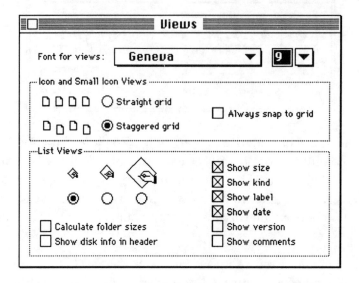

Instead of the boring old 9-point Geneva we've been stuck with since 1984, the **Font for views** area at the top of this box lets you select any font and font size available to your Mac for text in Finder windows or in the names of icons on the desktop. (But you can't change the fonts used for window titles or menu names in the menu bar.)

To change the font, click on the font name to display a pop-up menu of fonts currently installed in your System file. Drag through the menu to choose one. To change the font size, click on the triangle next to that box and select one from the menu of sizes available. As soon as you select a different font or size, the change takes place immediately.

In the **Icon and Small Icon Views** area, you can now choose either straight or staggered icon layouts in Finder windows. The examples next to the *Straight grid* and *Staggered grid* buttons show how icons are arranged in each case when you choose the *Clean Up Window* command on the Special menu. Clicking the *Staggered grid* button helps you squeeze more icons into a window without having their names overlap.

The *Always snap to grid* checkbox forces the icons in a window to be on the straight or staggered grid you have chosen. When this box is checked, it's impossible to drag an icon off the grid. You can temporarily reverse this checkbox's current setting by holding down ⌘ when you drag an icon.

In the **List Views** area, the three buttons under the different-sized icons let you pick what size icon will appear next to item names in list views. Normally this is the smallest of the three, but if you've used custom icons, you might want to select a larger size so you can see them more clearly.

This area also lets you control the amount of information displayed about each item in a list view window. With the standard settings, you see the name, kind, label, date and size information, like this:

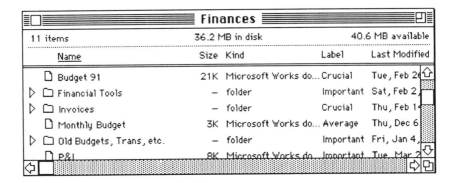

The item's name will always appear, but now you can choose whether you want the other categories in the list view window—size, kind, label, date, version and comments—by checking or unchecking the relevant *Show...* box.

Here's what a window looks like with only the *Show kind* box checked:

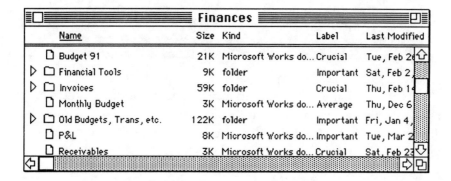

These options help you make more efficient use of desktop space. In the above example, hiding the size, label and date information lets you make the window a lot narrower.

The *Calculate folder sizes* checkbox tells the Mac to determine the size of each folder's contents and display it in the list view window, like this:

	Name	Size	Kind	Label	Last Modified
	Budget 91	21K	Microsoft Works do...	Crucial	Tue, Feb 26
▷	Financial Tools	9K	folder	Important	Sat, Feb 2
▷	Invoices	59K	folder	Crucial	Thu, Feb 14
	Monthly Budget	3K	Microsoft Works do...	Average	Thu, Dec 6
▷	Old Budgets, Trans, etc.	122K	folder	Important	Fri, Jan 4
	P&L	8K	Microsoft Works do...	Important	Tue, Mar 2
	Receivables	3K	Microsoft Works do...	Crucial	Sat, Feb 23

You'll see that under the Size category for folders, the total size of the folder and its contents appears instead of just a dash. If there are a lot of folders on your disk, using this option can slow down screen response considerably, because the Mac calculates folder sizes each time you change or open a window.

The *Show disk info in header* checkbox displays a disk's occupied space and free space just under a window's title bar, like this:

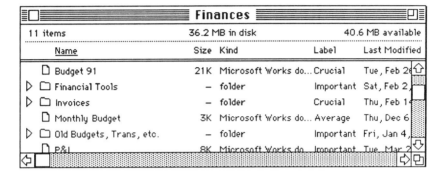

Under older system software versions, you had to switch to icon view for this information, but now you can see it in any window.

Other new control panels

The remaining five control panels found in the Control Panels folder are also new with System 7. They're listed below and are covered in detail in the chapters that describe the System 7 features they relate to.

Labels

Labels are a new way to identify documents, programs or folders in Finder windows. A label is a name and—on color Macs—a color or shade that you can attach to any item on the desktop or in a Finder window. These labels appear in a new Labels column in list view windows of the Finder.

This control panel and the procedure for changing labels are covered in more detail in Chapter 6 under *Customizing labels*, p. 79.

Memory

The Memory control panel lets you control the cache size, virtual memory and 32-bit addressing of your Mac. It's covered in detail in Chapter 9 in the section *Managing program memory*, p. 122.

File Sharing Monitor

This control panel shows you which folders or disks you're sharing over an AppleTalk network, and which other users on an AppleTalk network are currently sharing folders you have made available from your disk.

You can't open the File Sharing Monitor unless you've turned on file sharing with the Sharing Setup control panel. For more information about the File Sharing Monitor, see Chapter 11.

Sharing Setup

The Sharing Setup control panel is where you turn on file sharing, identify yourself and your Mac to the network, and control program linking. These topics are covered in Chapters 12–14.

Users & Groups

When you use file sharing or program linking on your Mac, you can limit access to specific users or groups of users on your network by using the Users & Groups control panel (and you can also restrict them to specific documents using the *Sharing...* command on the Finder's File menu). This procedure is covered in detail in Chapter 12.

WORKING WITH APPLICATIONS

Chapter 9
Using applications

Managing program memory **122**

Opening & saving documents **127**

Using stationery **130**

Publishing and subscribing **133**

System 7 brings several changes to the way you work with applications. We'll look first at some minor changes in how you manage the memory they use. Next we'll consider those changes to the Mac's hierarchical file system that affect how you open or save files from within applications. Finally, we'll take a quick look at System 7's new publish and subscribe capability and what that will mean for applications that support it.

Managing program memory

Now that MultiFinder's features are built into System 7, you'll probably find yourself running more than one program at a time, even if you never used MultiFinder before. This may cause you to exceed the amount of memory that's been set aside for each program. If you open a lot of documents at once with one program, or if you work with particularly large documents, you'll usually get a warning that you need to close some. Sometimes, though, the program will quit without warning.

In this section we'll look at four ways to manage your Mac's available memory, so you can run as many applications or open as many documents as possible.

Resetting the current memory

In Chapter 5 there's a detailed discussion of how to use *Get Info* on the File menu to increase an application's memory allocation on p. 62 under *The Get Info command.*

Using the Memory control panel

The other three techniques for managing memory on your Mac are all handled with the **Memory** control panel in the Control Panels folder. Just doubleclick it to open it, and you'll see a control panel like this:

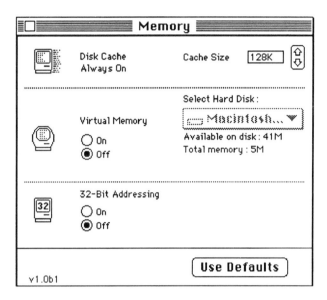

If your Mac can't use virtual memory or 32-bit addressing, your Memory control panel won't display all three sections shown here.

Adjusting the disk cache

For several years, Mac system software has let you turn on a RAM cache, a portion of memory that's set aside to hold frequently used data. That way, the data doesn't have to be read from disk every time you need it, which can significantly speed up operation of your system software and applications. In System 7, it's called the **disk cache**, and you allocate its size here in the Memory control panel.

In System 6 you could turn the cache on or off as well as set its size (using the General icon in the Control Panel). But, apparently, so much system software is now swapped between the disk and memory during a session with your Mac, performance would be too slow without help from the cache. So in System 7, it's on all the time.

To adjust the size of the disk cache, use the arrows on the right. In System 7, it can't be set less than 16K and you'll see a default size from 32K up, depending on which Mac you're using and how much RAM you have. If your Mac has relatively little RAM and you want to grab as much of it as possible for running applications, make the disk cache as small as possible. This may cause a slowdown in system software performance, but it will give you the space to run the maximum number of applications.

The change in cache size doesn't take place until you restart your Mac.

Using virtual memory

With the sizes of programs increasing as they are, available memory in a Mac is in shorter supply than ever. If you're using a 68030-based Mac, a Mac LC or a 68020-based Mac with the optional PMMU (Paged Memory Management Unit) chip, you can take advantage of System 7's **virtual memory** feature to run more applications. Virtual memory lets your Mac set aside unused space on a hard disk and treat it as RAM. (**Note:** Apple doesn't officially support third-party accelerator cards with 68020 processors and PMMU chips, but these products will probably have some sort of fix to make them fully compatible with System 7. Check with your accelerator card's manufacturer.)

Even if your Mac will let you use virtual memory, it's probably not something you should do every day. Since it's really space on your hard disk, programs or data stored in virtual memory are accessed at disk speed, which is much slower than RAM. If you have enough RAM (four megabytes or more), you may not notice the performance decrease, unless you switch from one large program to another and they are swapped between memory space on the disk and your Mac's RAM. But you'll definitely notice a slowdown if you only have two megabytes of RAM.

Here's how to use it:

1. Open the Memory control panel. It will contain options for using virtual memory only if your Mac can use it.

2. Click the *On* button in the Virtual Memory section. The hard disk name becomes active and the *After restart* setting appears below the Total memory indicator, like this:

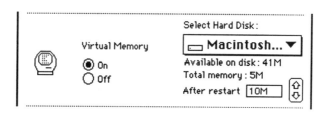

(If you didn't update your hard disk driver when you installed System 7, a message box will tell you to do so now. Restart your Mac with the Utilities disk that contains the Apple HD SC Setup program, open the program and click the *Update* button.)

Available on disk tells you how much free space there is on the hard disk named in the box above. (If you have more than one hard disk connected to your Mac, you can click on the disk name and choose another one from the pop-up menu that appears.) **Total memory** shows how much RAM is installed in your Mac. The *After restart* box tells you how much real RAM and virtual memory combined you will have after you restart your Mac.

When you turn virtual memory on, the Mac automatically matches your RAM. In this case, it sets up five megabytes of virtual memory to equal the five megabytes of RAM, for a total of ten megabytes.

3. Click one of the arrows next to *After restart* to set a different amount of virtual memory, if you like. Remember, the figure shown here is your actual RAM plus virtual memory.

After you turn on virtual memory and restart, System 7 creates a file in your System Folder called **VM Storage**. Its size is determined by the *After restart* amount (not just the amount of virtual memory). So your hard disk must have at least as much free space as the *After restart* box shows. Furthermore, the space must be contiguous (in one large block of space on the disk), not fragmented (the sum of several smaller blocks of free space). The control panel won't let you set up more virtual memory than your available disk space allows.

4. Close the Memory control panel and restart the Mac.

Here are a couple of tips for making the most of virtual memory:

- You really need four megabytes of RAM for it to run smoothly, though it's possible to run it with fewer.

- It may not be compatible with some programs—those which insist on being in genuine RAM rather than virtual memory.

- Virtual memory works faster if you use it for several smaller programs than for one big program.

- Don't set up more virtual memory than you have RAM. If you have five megabytes of RAM, set up five megabytes or less of virtual memory. The Mac runs even more slowly if you try to use more virtual memory than you have RAM.

Using 32-bit addressing

If you have a Mac IIci, IIsi, LC, IIfx or a newer model based on the 68030 or 68040 chips, **32-bit addressing** lets you exploit a lot more RAM in your Mac. (This is mainly useful if you work with very large files, or you want to be able to load dozens of programs at a time.) These newer Macs can use 32-bit numbers to specify memory addresses (as opposed to 16-bit numbers on other Macs), so they can handle far more memory locations and therefore use much more RAM (for exactly how much more, check the Special Features manual that came with your Mac). For example, while a Mac Classic can address a maximum of four megabytes of RAM, a Mac IIfx with 32-bit addressing can address up to 128 megabytes of RAM. Of course, you have to buy and install extra RAM in order to use it.

To turn on 32-bit addressing:

1. Open the Memory control panel. If your Mac supports 32-bit addressing, you'll see a section for turning it on at the bottom of the window, like this:

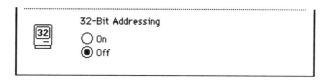

2. Click the *On* button. You'll see a message to the right of the buttons that says *32-bit address is off (will be on after restart)*.

3. Close the control panel and restart your Mac.

Opening & saving documents

System 7 makes three changes to how you open and save documents. There's a new level of organization in the file structure, above the disk drive level, called the desktop. It's visible in both dialog boxes and other directory paths. Secondly, in some directory dialog boxes you'll also notice a *New Folder* button. Finally, there's a new stationery feature that lets you easily create template documents for any program.

The Desktop level and button

In the Finder, the desktop is the place where you can see at a glance all the disks, network servers or shared folders you currently have available, along with the Trash and any program or document icons you've moved to the desktop. Before System 7, there was no way to see everything on the Finder's desktop from inside a directory dialog box. You had to click the *Drive* button to switch from the contents of one drive to another.

In System 7, the desktop now shows up as the highest organizational level in lists like directory paths and dialog boxes, better reflecting the role it plays in the Finder. This makes it much easier to work with several disks at once.

When you open or save a new document from inside an application under System 7, you'll see the familiar directory dialog box, with the *Drive* button replaced by the **Desktop** button. Clicking the *Desktop* button moves you to the Desktop level, like this:

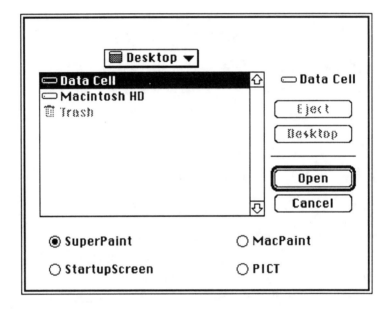

The name above the list box has changed to Desktop, and the list itself now shows the disks or other storage locations currently on the desktop.

The name of the disk you're on is still shown above the *Eject* button at the right. To switch disks, just doubleclick a different one in the list. (Dimmed items aren't available. The trash is dimmed above because this is an *Open* dialog box in SuperPaint, and there's nothing in the Trash for it to open.)

The Desktop level also appears below the disk name on every directory path you display in a pop-up menu, like this:

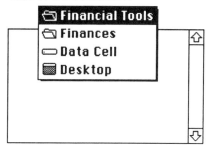

The New Folder button

Another change to the directory dialog box is the *New Folder* button. When you use *Save* with a new document, or whenever you use *Save As...*, the directory dialog box may (if your application supports it) contain a *New Folder* button, like this:

Making a new folder from inside a directory dialog box is obviously useful, and you'll soon see this button supported in most applications.

Using stationery

Some applications already have a stationery feature that lets you save a formatted template and then open it as a new untitled document, instead of having to re-create letterhead or re-set margins all the time. System 7 makes **stationery** possible for any program.

For instance, you might create stationery that stores your name and address in a nice font. Then, whenever you open that piece of stationery you'll have a new untitled page with your letterhead already on it.

Making stationery in the Save As... box

If your application supports this new feature, *Save As...* will let you create stationery (if not, you can still use this feature from the Finder—see the next section). System 7's TeachText utility has a good preview of what this feature will look like when other developers support it in their programs. It uses a new icon created by Apple that looks like a stationery pad.

To see for yourself, open TeachText (or, if it's open, choose *New* from the File menu), type a couple of characters and then choose *Save* from the File menu. At the lower right corner of the directory dialog box that appears, you'll see the icons and the buttons you click to save the file as a standard document or as stationery, like this:

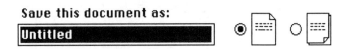

The stationery icon is the one on the right—the one that looks like a page being lifted off a pad.

Making stationery in the Finder

If your application doesn't offer a stationery option in the Save As... dialog box, you can use the Finder to make any document into a stationery pad. Here's how:

1. Select the document you want to make into a stationery pad by clicking on it in the Finder.

2. Choose *Get Info* from the File menu (other information about *Get Info* is covered in Chapter 5, p. 61). You'll see an information window like this:

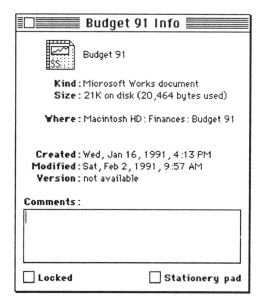

Notice that the icon and the Kind information show that this is a Microsoft Works document.

3. Check the ***Stationery pad*** checkbox at the bottom of the window. The document icon changes into a stationery pad and the Kind information changes with it, like this:

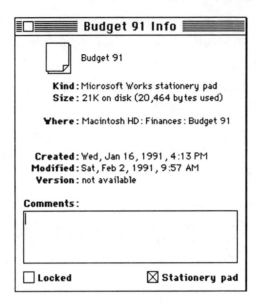

4. Close the window.

The next time you doubleclick this document in the Finder to open it, you'll see a message that asks you to name the new document, like this:

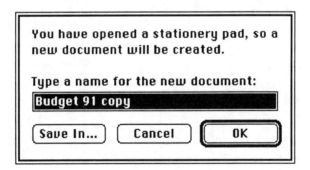

Once you name the document and click *OK*, the new document will appear with all the formatting and text you saved in the stationery pad. You can also save the template to another location—clicking the *Save In...* button produces a directory dialog box.

Changing a stationery pad

If you'd like to change the text or formatting of a stationery pad document, here's what you do:

1. First, open the program you used to create the stationery document, and then open the stationery document. You'll see a message like this:

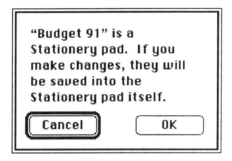

2. Click *OK*. The document will open.

3. Make the changes you want and then save the file. It will be saved back to your disk as the stationery pad.

Publishing and subscribing

Publishing and subscribing are powerful new capabilities in System 7 that will make life a lot easier for Mac users who regularly copy data from one document to another. These features may not be available to you when you first install System 7—each application must specifically support publishing and subscribing, and it will probably take a few months for software publishers to update their products. But eventually, most will support this new feature, so we'll take a look at it here.

What's publishing and subscribing?

Publishing and subscribing allows you to create continuous, automatic data connections between copies of the same data—within the same document or in different documents, on your own Mac or on a network. You select data and "publish" it from one document and "subscribe" to that data in another document (or in another place in the same document). After that, every change to that data in the publishing document will also show up in the subscribing document.

Publish and subscribe takes cutting and pasting to a new level. With cut and paste, you select data in one document and copy or cut it to the Clipboard. Then you select another location, in that document or another one, and paste the data there. This is like taking a snapshot of a painting in progress and sending it to someone. As soon as you change the painting, the snapshot is out of date.

With publish and subscribe, you select data in one document and publish it (make it available for use elsewhere) by creating an **edition**, a special file that always contains a current copy of the published data. Once you've created an edition file, you can subscribe to that edition from other documents. Because the edition always contains the most recent version of the published data, a subscriber to the edition always has a current version of the data. Change the data in the original publishing document, and the data in the subscribing document changes automatically.

This has lots of possibilities. Suppose two people produce a monthly report, for example. The person responsible for a graph might publish the graph, and then the person responsible for the report's layout could subscribe to the graph. Whenever new data came in each month, the graph person would update the graph on his Macintosh. Because the graph is published, the layout person's version of the graph would automatically be updated to reflect the new data.

Particular uses for publish and subscribe will depend, of course, on how developers support it in their programs. But this feature will undoubtedly become a nearly universal enhancement to Mac programs, as commonplace as the Clipboard.

Publishing and subscribing in action

Each application will add its own wrinkles to publishing and subscribing, but here's the basic process so you'll be familiar with it when it arrives. (This is using Apple's prerelease version of System 7, which came with sample writing and drawing programs that have the new features. These programs, though, won't be offered for sale.)

Suppose you've created something in the draw program that you want to use in a word processor document.

1. Select the drawing or the portion of it you want to publish, like this:

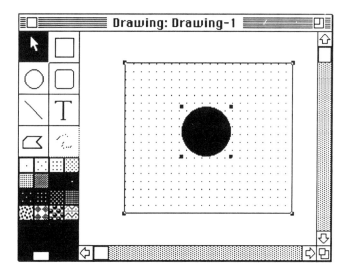

2. Choose **Create Publisher...** from the Edit menu. A directory dialog box appears, like this:

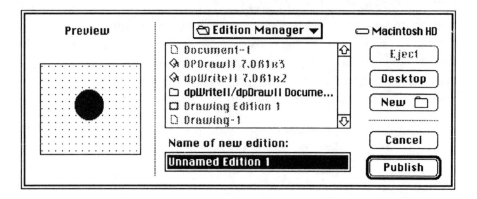

The dialog box includes a preview of the data you've selected for publication—in this case the drawing. The file you're creating is an edition, which is why the entry box for the file name is headed *Name of new edition.* (This file has nothing to do with the document that contains your data—in this case a draw document. It contains only the data you selected.)

3. Type a name for the edition file and click *Publish*. The edition is saved to disk.

4. Open the word processor document and move the insertion point to the place where you want the drawing to appear.

5. Choose *Subscribe to...* from the Edit menu. A directory dialog box appears, like this:

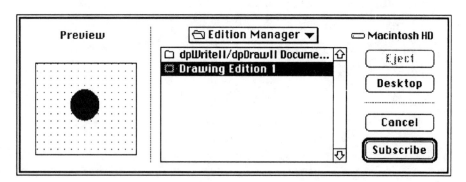

6. Navigate to the edition file that contains the drawing and doubleclick it, or select it and click *Subscribe*. The drawing appears in the document, like this:

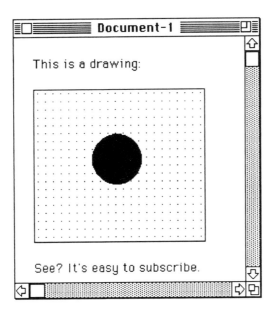

Now that the edition is published and the word processor document has subscribed to it, any changes to the original drawing—say, making the circle gray—will show up in the word processor's subscription.

Publisher and subscriber options

In addition to the basic functions, there will be publish and subscribe options. For example, here's the dialog box I got when I chose **Subscriber Options...** from the Edit menu in Apple's sample word processing program:

Use *Subscriber* to find the edition file to which you've subscribed—the pop-up menu shows the edition file name and its directory path. You can also cancel the subscription, open the publishing document, and choose to update the subscriber data from the edition file manually instead. (Maintaining an automatic link between two documents can slow down the Mac's operation, especially if the two linked documents are on different hard disks on a network.)

Finally, because you're creating a data link between two documents, there will be a slew of new alert boxes that will warn you about deleting published data from a document or deleting a published edition file, since these kinds of changes can affect other documents as well.

This gives you only a glimpse of what's to come with publishing and subscribing on the Mac. But even so, you can see this new feature will make it a lot easier to transfer information between documents.

WORKING WITH APPLICATIONS

Chapter 10
Printing

The three font formats **140**

Printing with an ImageWriter **141**

Printing with a LaserWriter **143**

Using PrintMonitor **147**

The LaserWriter Font Utility **153**

Mixing TrueType and
  other fonts on a LaserWriter **159**

System 7 consolidates and extends several recent changes in Macintosh printing. Unless you bought a Mac or a LaserWriter after early 1990, many of these changes will be new to you. In this chapter, we'll cover them and we'll also look at the new TrueType fonts and how they work on both ImageWriter and LaserWriter printers.

The three font formats

There are essentially three font formats or types of font available for Macintosh screen display and printing:

- Fixed-size, or bitmapped fonts come in specific sizes like Geneva 14. With these fonts, each character is made up of a series of dots. This was the first Mac font format, and it's the one still used for most Mac screen fonts. You can also buy such fonts from companies other than Apple.

    The problem with fixed-size fonts is that you need to install a different font file for each size you want to display faithfully on your screen. Otherwise the Mac will shrink or enlarge a different-sized font that you do have installed, making the characters look blocky or blurred (and, sometimes, hard to read).

- Outline fonts are scalable—the font is stored as a mathematical description, and its characters are reproduced clearly at whatever size you specify. You only need one outline file on your Mac for each font family you want to use. Outline font files are also smaller—one file might be 50K or so, while a collection of bitmapped files for one font could use up 100–200K on your disk.

    The problem here is that while LaserWriter printers support the Postscript outline format, the Mac screen and the ImageWriter don't. So even though you might need only one Helvetica file for printing on your LaserWriter, you still need a handful of fixed-size, bitmapped Helvetica files to display different sizes accurately on your screen, or print them clearly on an ImageWriter. If you don't have *any* fixed-size Helvetica files installed, you won't even be able to select the font from a menu.

- **TrueType** fonts are scalable *and* they can be displayed on the Mac screen. You need only one file—the same one for screen display and for printing—for each font family. You can specify any font size you like, and it will come out looking smooth on both the screen and the printer. This is the way Mac fonts should have worked all along.

System 7 comes with both fixed-size and TrueType fonts. You can use either kind, or even mix them in the same document. As more TrueType fonts become available, though, you'll probably want to switch over to them. Besides giving you better quality, it's a lot easier to manage a single scalable file for each font family than to deal with several files for different font sizes.

(For instructions on installing fonts, see *The System File: installing fonts and sounds* in Chapter 7, p. 99.)

Now, let's see how these formats work on the Mac and its printers.

Printing with an ImageWriter

If you use an ImageWriter or another dot-matrix printer that uses the ImageWriter printer driver, the only thing new with System 7 is TrueType fonts. Printing procedures haven't changed for ImageWriter users in a couple of years, and the dialog boxes you see when you choose *Page Setup...* and *Print...* from the File menu are the same.

TrueType fonts, however, will make your printouts look better compared with those you got with fixed-size fonts.

Printing with fixed-size fonts

Like the Mac's screen, the ImageWriter can produce smooth text only if your Mac supplies the font in exactly the size you specify. The ImageWriter takes that font and size from your System file and reproduces it as a bit map (a collection of dots) on paper.

If you specify a font size that isn't installed in your System file, the Mac makes a guess, based on a size that *is*, at what the characters would look like. Usually, the guess isn't very good—the characters come out looking blocky instead of smooth.

Furthermore, the ImageWriter prints its Best-quality text by requesting a double-sized font from the Mac and having the Mac shrink it to the size you want, which makes each letter look darker and smoother on paper. If you want Best-quality Geneva 12, for example, you need Geneva 24 installed in your System file.

So fixed-size fonts severely limit your options for producing good quality printing on an ImageWriter. The fixed-size fonts supplied with the system software only come in 9, 10, 12, 14, 18, 20 and 24 point sizes, so if you need to use a size like 11 or 36 points, the characters won't look right.

Printing with TrueType fonts

With TrueType fonts, the Mac scales the font to whatever size you specify, so whether it's 11, 13, 36, 48, 50 or 72 point type, the ImageWriter always gets an exact-sized sample to print from. As a result, TrueType characters in any size look as smooth as those you'd get from a fixed-size font. When you use Best-quality printing, the font is automatically scaled to twice the specified size and then reduced 50% so the ImageWriter can print a denser, sharper character.

Printing with a LaserWriter

For LaserWriter users, System 7 incorporates changes to the *Print...* command's dialog box, the PrintMonitor program and the LaserWriter Font Utility. We'll look at these changes here. We'll also look at using TrueType fonts on a LaserWriter.

The Page Setup... dialog box

The *Page Setup...* dialog box in System 7 is just like the one in System 6, except for the pop-up menu in the paper selection area. When you choose *Page Setup...* from the File menu in the Finder, this dialog box appears:

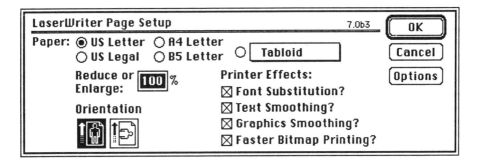

(It may contain some extra options when you choose *Page Setup...* from inside an application. Many applications, including Word and PageMaker, offer options for printing PostScript information from a file.)

In the set of *Paper* options at the top of the box, you'll notice the new pop-up menu that says *Tabloid* (which is like the one in System 6's *Page Setup...* box for color or grayscale printing). Use it to choose other paper sizes, such as envelopes. The original LaserWriter had trouble printing anything except 8-1/2 x 11" sheets, but today's LaserWriters can easily accept various paper sizes and envelopes.

As before, *Reduce or Enlarge* lets you print a document's contents in a smaller or larger size.

As before, the *Orientation* icons let you print a document vertically (standard) or sideways on the page. (Note, however, that the sideways option makes printing slower because the LaserWriter has to take extra time to flip the document's contents before printing them.)

The *Printer Effects* options are all checked when you first open the *Page Setup...* dialog box. Here's what they do:

Font Substitution tells the LaserWriter to substitute three of its built-in fonts for certain ones you specify on your screen, rather than print bitmap versions of the screen fonts. If the *Font Substitution* box is checked, the LaserWriter will substitute Helvetica for Geneva, Times for New York and Courier for Monaco.

Text Smoothing and *Graphics Smoothing* tell the LaserWriter to try to eliminate rough edges from type or graphics. Neither seems to cause print jobs to take longer, so you might as well leave them checked.

Faster Bitmap Printing preprocesses bitmapped images before they're sent to the LaserWriter. You can leave this box checked too, since it doesn't seem to hurt the printer's performance.

More Page Setup options

Finally, when you click the *Options* button on the right, you get another dialog box, like this (it's unchanged from System 6's):

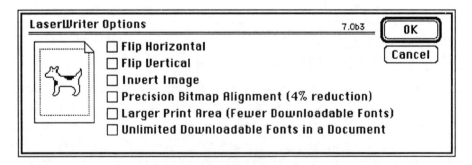

What's nice about this dialog box is that you can see how each option will affect your document by looking at the sample on the left. None of these options is checked when you first display the dialog box.

Flip Horizontal and *Flip Vertical* do what they say—flip the entire image on your page either horizontally or vertically.

Invert Image creates a negative of your document, swapping white for black on the page.

Precision Bitmap Alignment reduces the whole page to 96% to avoid distortion when a bitmapped screen image on your Mac is converted to the LaserWriter's 300dpi resolution.

Larger Print Area When you check this box, you'll be able to print closer to the edges of your paper (although certain applications won't let you).

Unlimited Downloadable Fonts Your LaserWriter can typically make use of only two or three downloadable fonts when printing a given document as each one eats up RAM. (Exactly how many depends on which LaserWriter model you have and how much memory it has.) When you check this box, you remove the limit on the number of fonts per document. Doing this, however, will really slow down printing.

The Print... dialog box

This dialog box now allows you to save your document to a PostScript file, rather than send it to the printer. Other than that, it's the same as in recent versions of System 6. But in case you're upgrading from an older version, we'll cover the whole box briefly.

When you choose *Print...* from the File menu, the dialog box looks like this:

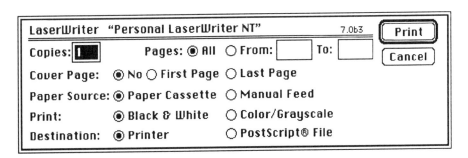

Like the *Page Setup...* dialog box, this one may also look different when you choose it from inside an application. Some programs add printing options of their own, like whether to print back to front (in reverse order). Most of the basic features shown above are unchanged from System 6.

Copies lets you specify how many copies of the document to print. The default setting here is one.

Pages lets you print either the entire document or a range of pages in it.

Cover Page tells the printer to print a one-page report detailing the user name, application, document name, printer name, the date and the time. Clicking *First Page* or *Last Page* prints the cover page before or after the actual document.

Paper Source lets you use either the *Paper Cassette* built into your printer or the *Manual Feed* slot (part of the *Multipurpose Tray* on newer LaserWriter models). If you choose *Manual Feed*, you'll be reminded to insert paper into the manual feed slot as the printing job begins. (You can turn this warning off with the *Preferences...* command in the PrintMonitor application. See below, p. 151.)

The *Print* buttons are primarily for people who have a color printer that uses the LaserWriter driver. Typically, you'll use the default *Black & White* option. If your printer can print in color, you must choose *Color/Grayscale* to do so. If you choose *Color/Grayscale* with a black and white printer, the printer will try reproducing color or grayscale images with halftones (by printing dot patterns at different densities to imitate different shades of gray).

Destination is a new feature that lets you send your document to the *Printer* or save it as a *PostScript® File*. With some graphics files, you'll get a better quality printout if you first save it as a PostScript file, because the LaserWriter prints finer, smoother lines and curves from PostScript instructions than it does by creating a bitmap of a drawing.

Many drawing programs have a built-in option to save files as PostScript files, but if yours doesn't, you can create a PostScript file this way. When you choose *PostScript File* here, the *Print* button changes to *Save*, and when you click it, you see a directory dialog box that lets you specify a disk and folder location for the new PostScript file.

Using PrintMonitor

If you're using an ImageWriter or another printer that doesn't have a LaserWriter printer driver, you can skip this section, since PrintMonitor only works with those that do (or with LaserWriters themselves, of course).

PrintMonitor is a utility program in your System Folder that lets your Mac handle print jobs in the background while you get on with other work. We'll cover all of its features and operations here. Even if you've used PrintMonitor before, you'll want to check out the new options available with the *Preferences...* command in the *PrintMonitor menu* section, p. 151 below.

Starting PrintMonitor

To print in the background, you have to set PrintMonitor to start up automatically. Here's the procedure:

1. Select the Chooser from the menu. The Chooser window appears.

2. Select the LaserWriter icon at the left side of the window. The LaserWriter name appears at the right, and the background printing options appear below the list of printer names, like this:

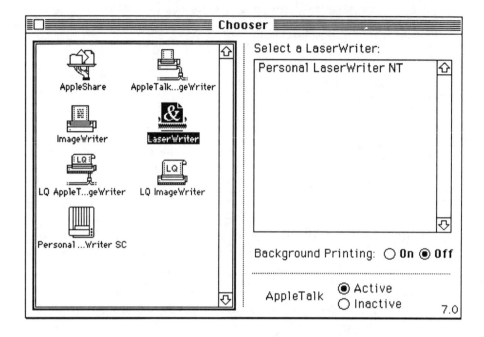

3. Click on the name of the LaserWriter you want to use, and then click the *On* button next to **Background Printing**.

4. Close the Chooser window.

Once you've turned on background printing, the Mac will automatically start up PrintMonitor whenever you print a document. Then your document is quickly sent to the PrintMonitor Documents folder (inside your System Folder), from which it's passed on to the printer while you get on with other work. More than one printing job can be in the background at once.

Once the printing job is done, the PrintMonitor program automatically quits.

You can also start PrintMonitor without printing a document by doubleclicking its icon inside the System Folder.

The PrintMonitor window

The PrintMonitor window shows the status and controls the operation of any printing jobs you've started. Normally this window is hidden when printing jobs are in progress, but you can display it in three ways:

- Change the PrintMonitor preferences to make the window appear during printing jobs (see *The PrintMonitor menu*, p. 151 below).

- Choose *PrintMonitor* from the Application menu when a printing job is in progress.

- Doubleclick on the PrintMonitor program to start it up when you aren't printing something.

The PrintMonitor window shows the status of the current printing job and any other jobs that are waiting to be printed. If you display the window by using the third option above, when there's no printing job underway and none waiting to be printed, it'll be empty, with none of the following options available.

Here's what the PrintMonitor window looks like when a printing job's underway and two documents are waiting to be printed:

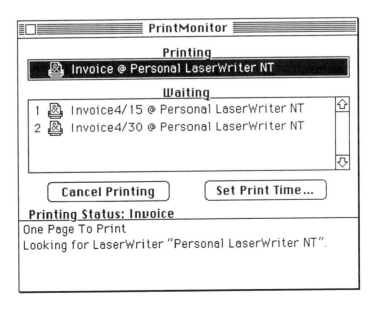

At the top of the window, the ***Printing*** box shows the name of the document currently being printed and the name of the LaserWriter being used. The ***Printing Status*** box shows the number of pages remaining to be printed in the current job and its status—just the same as the messages that would pop up on your screen during a printing job if you had background printing turned off (*Looking for LaserWriter...*, *starting job*, etc.).

The ***Cancel Printing*** button cancels the current job.

The ***Waiting*** list shows the names of two documents waiting to print, numbered in the order they will be printed. You can use this list to view information about a document, change the order of documents or remove a document so it doesn't print at all:

- To view information about a document, select its name on the waiting list. The *Printing Status* box will show which program created the document, when the document was spooled into the PrintMonitor Documents folder on your disk, and how many pages it contains.

- To change the printing order on the waiting list, select the printer icon between the document's name and number and drag it to a different place on the list, which will then be renumbered from top to bottom.

- To remove a document from the waiting list, select it and click the ***Remove from List*** button that appears underneath the waiting list.

Set Print Time... lets you delay printing of a particular job. When you click this button, the Print Time dialog box appears, like this:

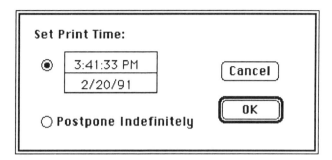

This box shows the print time and date of the document that is currently printing, or one you've selected on the waiting list. You can click in the time or date boxes to change them, or click the *Postpone Indefinitely* button to put off a printing job until further notice.

PrintMonitor alerts

When your printer has a problem, the Mac normally displays an alert box. You'll get one when the paper jams, or you run out of paper, or you're being reminded to insert paper in the manual feed tray.

When you're running PrintMonitor, you can choose whether these alerts pop up on top of the work you're currently doing, or whether they just cause the PrintMonitor icon to flash in the menu bar, by using the *Preferences...* command on the PrintMonitor menu, which is described next.

The PrintMonitor menu

Whenever the PrintMonitor is running, it has its own File menu in the menu bar, which looks like this:

Open displays the PrintMonitor window, and *Close* puts it away.

Stop Printing interrupts a printing job. After you select it, the command on the menu changes to *Resume Printing*, and choosing it restarts the job where it left off.

When you choose *Preferences...*, you'll see a dialog box like this:

```
Preferences...
   Show the PrintMonitor window when printing:
         ● No    ○ Yes
   When a printing error needs to be reported:
         ◆ ○ Only display ◆ in Application menu
         ◆ ● Also display icon in menu bar
         ◆ ○ Also display alert
   When a manual feed job starts:
         ○ Give no notification
         ◆ ● Display icon in menu bar
         ◆ ○ Also display alert

                              [ Cancel ]  [[ OK ]]
```

This example shows the default settings for these options.

Show the PrintMonitor window when printing Normally the PrintMonitor window is hidden when you're printing documents. If you really want the PrintMonitor window to show during printing jobs, click *Yes* here.

When a printing error needs to be reported As set above, the PrintMonitor icon will flash at the top of the Application menu whenever there's a printing problem. And when you open the Application menu, you'll see a diamond next to the PrintMonitor name. Once you select PrintMonitor from the menu in these situations, the actual alert box will overlay the PrintMonitor window, so you can deal with it.

It's a good idea to have the icon flash in the menu bar so at least you know there's a printing problem. But if you'd rather be kept in the dark, click *Only display* ♦ *in Application menu*. Then you'll have to check your printer or the Application menu to find out if there's a problem.

If you always want to deal with printer problems immediately, click the *Also display alert* button to display printer alert boxes on top of whatever else you're doing.

With either of the two bottom choices in *When a manual feed job starts* clicked, whenever you choose *Manual Feed* in the *Print...* command's dialog box and try to begin printing, the Mac starts flashing the icon in the menu bar or immediately displays an alert box (depending on your clicked choice) reminding you to insert paper in the manual feed tray. You have to click *OK* before printing will actually start.

If all this seems like a lot of hassle—and it is—click **Give no notification**. This will suspend the manual feed alert entirely, even if you're not using PrintMonitor for background printing. You'll still become aware of the problem if you forget to put paper in the manual feed tray, because the yellow "paper out" light on your LaserWriter will light up and your document won't print.

The LaserWriter Font Utility

The LaserWriter Font Utility (we'll just call it the Font Utility from here on) has been included with LaserWriter printers since 1989, but it's now included in the System 7 software as well.

LaserWriters have been improved a lot since the old LaserWriter and LaserWriter Plus, and the Font Utility lets you manage all their features more easily: download, list, display and print fonts, cancel the printer's startup page and many other useful things.

All of the Font Utility's features are controlled with menu commands. When you start up the program, you see a dialog box that explains the program's basic purpose. After you click the *OK* button, the Mac checks to see what kind of LaserWriter you have and which fonts are installed in it, and then the Font Utility's File, Edit and Utilities menus appear in the menu bar.

File menu commands

The File menu contains commands for downloading, displaying and printing fonts, among other things. It looks like this:

```
File
 Download Fonts...         ⌘D
 Display Available Fonts... ⌘L
 Initialize Printer's Disk...
 ─────────────────────────────
 Page Setup...
 Print Font Catalog...     ⌘P
 Print Font Samples...
 ─────────────────────────────
 Quit                      ⌘Q
```

The ***Download Fonts...*** command produces a dialog box like this:

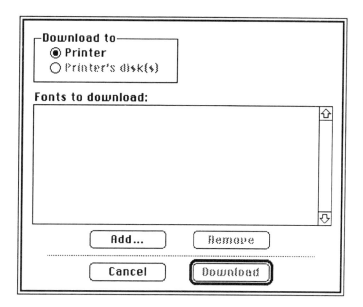

Here you can select one or more fonts from your disk and then download them all to your printer at once.

The *Download to* buttons let you choose whether to download your selected fonts to the printer or to the printer's hard disk—if it has one directly connected. (If it doesn't, you only have the option of downloading to the printer, as in the above example.)

The **Fonts to download** list shows what fonts you've selected for downloading.

To choose a font for downloading, click the *Add...* button. You'll see a standard directory dialog box you can use to navigate to and select a font file. Once you've done so and clicked the box's *Open* button, the font file's name is added to this list here.

The *Remove* button lets you delete fonts from the list to be downloaded. Just select the font file name and click the *Remove* button.

When you've collected all the fonts you want to download in the list box, click the **Download** button to send them to the printer.

When you choose **Display available fonts...** from the File menu, the program lists all the fonts currently available to your printer. You'll see a window like this:

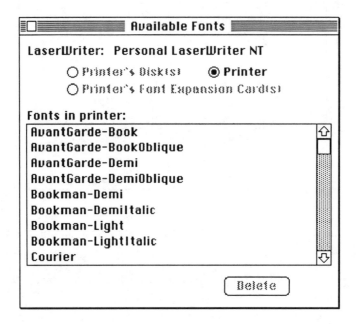

If you have a hard disk or expansion card connected to your printer, you'll be able to list the fonts they store by clicking the relevant button; otherwise, their buttons will be dimmed, as shown.

The list of fonts shows all the fonts in your printer, whether they're built-in or downloaded. If it shows any downloaded fonts, you can select them and click the **Delete** button to remove them from the Printer's memory, disk or expansion card.

If you have a hard disk connected to your printer, you use the **Initialize Printer's Disk...** command on the File menu to initialize it. You must use this command to format your LaserWriter's hard disk since it needs to be formatted differently from hard disks connected to your Mac.

The *Page Setup...* command on the File menu produces the standard LaserWriter Page Setup dialog box. *Print Font Catalog...* prints a list of the fonts available to your printer, and *Print Font Samples...* also prints that list, along with a sample of each font. (Since it uses all the fonts in your printer, the Font Samples list takes a while to print.)

Edit menu commands

The Font Utility's Edit menu contains the same commands as the Edit menu in the Finder. You don't need them when you're using the Font Utility.

Utilities menu commands

The Utilities menu looks like this:

```
Utilities
Download PostScript File...
Start Page Options...
Remove TrueType...
Restart Printer...
```

The *Download PostScript File...* command lets you select a PostScript file from your disk and send it to the LaserWriter for printing. Choosing this command displays a directory dialog box where you can locate and select the file you want to print.

Once you select a file and click the *Open* button, you'll see another directory dialog box where you can name the output file created by the printing operation, if there is one. (If your PostScript file contains a series of PostScript commands, an output file is created at the end of the printing job listing all the PostScript commands that were executed.) After you click the *Save* button to save the output file, the PostScript file is downloaded to your LaserWriter and printed. If there has been no output file created at the end of the print job, you'll see a message telling you this.

If you select a non-PostScript file for printing with *Download PostScript File...*, nothing will happen when you try to print it. (The PrintMonitor program doesn't support PostScript files, so you have to wait until your PostScript file is printed before you can do any other work.)

The ***Start Page Options...*** command lets you decide whether your LaserWriter will print a startup page each time you turn it on. The startup page shows how many fonts are installed in your printer, how much memory it has, which version of PostScript it is using and, most importantly, how many pages it has printed. You probably don't need to see these statistics every time you turn on your printer, so you might as well save some paper by turning the page off.

When you choose *Start Page Options...*, you'll see a small dialog box where you can choose either *On* or *Off*. The standard setting is *On*, which means the printer will print a startup page. Click the *Off* button to do away with the startup page, then click the *OK* button to close the dialog box. Click the *On* button to turn the startup page on again.

The ***Remove TrueType...*** command removes all TrueType fonts from a LaserWriter's disk. If this command is dimmed (as in the example above) it's because you're not connected to a LaserWriter, the LaserWriter doesn't have a disk connected to it, the disk doesn't contain any TrueType fonts, or the printer isn't available.

The ***Restart Printer...*** command lets you reinitialize your printer, which is like turning it off and then back on again, except that you don't use the power switch. When you do this, you clear any downloaded fonts out of the printer's memory—you'll see a dialog box warning you about this when you choose this command. Click the ***Restart*** button to start up again. This will usually clear up any problems you have with the printer not executing print jobs correctly. (Sometimes, for example, the printer goes into a "preparing data" sequence indefinitely, and restarting it is the only way to clear out its buffer and get it working right again.)

Mixing TrueType and other fonts on a LaserWriter

System 7's new TrueType fonts give you more ways to produce nice-looking text on a LaserWriter, and they make it a lot easier to manage font files on your Mac. Some TrueType fonts are included with System 7 along with the same old fixed-size fonts we've had for years. To see which fonts of each type are installed in your System file, doubleclick on the System file icon in the System Folder. (For more information about this, see *Playing sounds and viewing fonts* in Chapter 7, p. 100.)

Built-in fonts and screen fonts

Your LaserWriter comes with about three dozen PostScript fonts built into its Read-Only Memory (ROM). These include various versions of Avant Garde, Courier, Times, Helvetica and Zapf Dingbats. Because they're built into your printer, these fonts can be used and printed more quickly than others.

But since the Macintosh's screen display doesn't support PostScript fonts, LaserWriters come with a floppy disk of screen fonts to match the printer's built-in ones. (You must install the screen fonts before you can select them from menus and see them on the screen.)

While the PostScript fonts can be printed smoothly at any size from about six points up to 128 points, the screen fonts only come in a range of fixed sizes (from about 9 points to 24 or sometimes 36 points). So there are lots of font sizes that print clearly, but don't display accurately.

But some of the LaserWriter's built-in fonts are now represented on the Mac's screen with the new TrueType fonts. You can scale *them* to any size you like, and they'll look almost as smooth on the screen as they will when printed—they're still not quite as smooth because the Mac screen has much lower resolution than the LaserWriter.

Downloadable fonts

There are hundreds of different fonts available besides the built-in LaserWriter fonts. You can use them on your LaserWriter by temporarily transferring (or *downloading*) them to the LaserWriter's RAM.

There two ways of doing this:

1. You can use the LaserWriter Font Utility to select and download fonts before you print a document. (The procedure is covered in *The LaserWriter Font Utility* on p. 153 of this chapter.) In this case, the font files can be stored anywhere on your disk, because you're the one who has to locate them and select them for downloading.

2. If you have downloadable fonts stored in your System Folder, the LaserWriter will ask the Mac to automatically look for them and download them when you print a document that uses those fonts. (But don't put them in a folder *within* the System Folder, or the printer won't find them.)

SHARING FILES AND LINKING PROGRAMS

Chapter 11
File sharing

File sharing for the AppleShare user **162**

File sharing step-by-step **164**

Connecting your Mac to other Macs **173**

File sharing lets people on a Mac network use files on each other's hard disks or CD-ROM disks. It's one of the most powerful new capabilities in System 7.

If you're an experienced AppleShare user and you're on an AppleTalk network, you can get up to speed on file sharing quickly by reading *File sharing for the AppleShare user* immediately following. But if you're not, start with *File sharing step-by-step* below.

File sharing for the AppleShare user

File sharing works very much like AppleShare—it turns your Mac into a network file server. But unlike an AppleShare server, a file-sharing Mac can still be used as an individual workstation. (When file sharing is on, it just uses an extra 200K of your Mac's available memory.) So any (or every) Mac on a network can both share its files and log onto other file-sharing Macs as a user.

Each file-sharing Mac has an **owner** who has complete control of all its files, much like the administrator of an AppleShare file server. As an owner, first you turn file sharing on, then you select the folder(s) or disk(s) you want to share and make them available for others to use. You can register users and groups and set access privileges for shared items just as you would on an AppleShare server. (See Chapter 12 for more on users, groups and access privileges.)

Connecting to other Macs to share their files is just like logging onto an AppleShare server. And as with AppleShare, you are the owner of every folder you create, whether it's on your disk or on another Mac.

The biggest difference between file sharing and AppleShare is ease of access. With file sharing, everything you select to share is open to everyone on the network—you must use access privileges to restrict availability. Under AppleShare, it's the opposite—each new folder on the shared disk is available only to its owner, who must specify who else may use it.

These differences will be obvious as you use file sharing.

Sharing your files with others

To turn file sharing on, open the **Sharing Setup** control panel in the Control Panels folder, enter your name, password and Mac name in the boxes shown, and then click the *Start* button under **File Sharing**. File sharing will start up in a few seconds and you can then close the Sharing Setup control panel.

On the desktop, select the folder or hard disk on your Macintosh that you want to share (you can't share floppy disks) and then choose *Sharing...* from the File menu. The sharing window appears.

In the sharing window, check the *Share this item and its contents* checkbox, then close the window. The item will now be available on the network.

You'll notice that as soon as you check the *Share this item...* checkbox, the access privileges options become active. For more on setting access privileges and registering users, see Chapter 12.

Monitoring and disconnecting users

To see who is connected to your Mac or to disconnect users, use the **File Sharing Monitor** control panel. It shows which folders you've made available for sharing and which users are currently sharing those items.

To disconnect a user, select the user's name in the **Connected Users** list and click the *Disconnect* button. You'll be able to set how much time will elapse before the user is disconnected, and a warning will appear on the user's Mac that this is about to take place.

To disconnect everyone at the same time, turn off file sharing by clicking the *Stop* button under File Sharing in the Sharing Setup control panel.

Connecting to other file-sharing Macs

You don't need to have file sharing on to use another Mac's shared folders or disks. File-sharing Macs become network file servers, and you connect to them the same way you log on to an AppleShare server. Click the AppleShare resource in the *Chooser*, and you'll see a list of other Macs on your network that are currently sharing files. Select the Mac you want, enter your user name and password if necessary, and then choose the folders or disks on the remote Mac that you want to add to your desktop.

File sharing step-by-step

File sharing on a network means being able to open and work with another Mac user's disks or folders (think of them as *shared items*) just as if they were your own—and, if you want, giving other users similar access to yours.

Until now, this required you to buy special networking software and perhaps an extra Mac and hard disk to function as a dedicated file server. Now, thanks to System 7, the same network you use to share a LaserWriter will let you share files.

When you have file sharing on, you're using an extra 200K of your Mac's available memory. You can share anything on hard disks or CD-ROM disks, with up to ten shared folders or disks on your desktop at once (although working with a shared item takes a bit longer than on a locally connected disk—that's why you can't share floppy disks over a network; the access times are too slow).

You can tell when your Mac is accessing data across the network because a pair of arrows blinks at the far left edge of your menu bar, like this:

The arrows disappear when the remote disk access is finished.

File sharing at a glance

How you use file sharing depends on whether you're sharing your own folders or disks with other users or accessing those items the owner of a remote Mac has made available for you to share.

If you're doing the latter—accessing someone else's shared items via your own Mac—you don't even need to turn file sharing on. You just connect to the remote Mac through *Chooser* and then select from the folders or disks the other Mac's owner has made available to you for sharing. Their icons appear on your desktop just as those of your unshared items would. And when you open the icon of the item you want access to, your Mac sends a signal over the network and opens the real disk or folder on the Mac that's sharing it.

When you share your folders with others on a network, however, you must turn file sharing on and select those items you want to share, and to what extent you want others to have access to them.

In order for this all to work, you have to be able to tell one Mac on the network from another. Before you can use a Mac for file sharing, you must register the Mac's name on the network. Each Mac must have a unique name.

Also, each Mac has an **owner**—a person who controls the file sharing functions on that Mac. You must register an owner name before you can use a Mac for file sharing.

Because a Mac might be used by more than one person, there are ways for other users who aren't Mac owners to share files. Users can register as anonymous guests or with a unique name. Users with unique names can have their own folders or disks on the network and can control who else can use them. (For more on registering users, see Chapter 12, p. 180.)

With System 7, you use various control panels, DAs and menu commands to set up your disk for file sharing, create users and grant them access privileges and connect to other file-sharing Macs. Let's look at the steps you take to set up a Mac for file sharing.

Setting up file sharing

Before you can use file sharing, there are three things you have to do:

- Connect your Mac to an AppleTalk network.
- Turn on AppleTalk on your Mac.
- Identify yourself and your Mac on the network.

(If you're already connected to a LaserWriter and some other Macs on a network, skip to *Identify yourself and your Mac* on the following page.)

Connect your Mac to a network It's beyond the scope of this book to examine options for physically connecting AppleTalk networks. If you're already connected to a LaserWriter, you're already on an AppleTalk network. If you don't yet have an AppleTalk network, you'll need to buy network connectors and cabling from your Apple dealer or a mail order company. The least expensive option for AppleTalk networking is ordinary telephone line cord and telephone network connectors that plug in between your Mac's printer port and the modular connector at the end of the telephone cord. See your Apple dealer or local user group for more information.

Turn on AppleTalk Once you're connected physically, you have to notify your system software about it. You do this with the *Chooser:*

1. Select the *Chooser* from the menu. The Chooser window opens (see top of next page).

2. Click the *Active* button in the lower right corner of the window to make AppleTalk active. You'll see a reminder about making sure you're really connected to an AppleTalk network. Click the *OK* button to make the reminder go away.

3. Close the Chooser window.

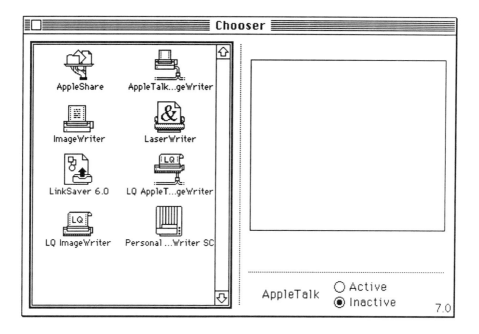

Identify yourself and your Mac This is handled with the **Sharing Setup** control panel.

1. Open Sharing Setup in the Control Panels folder. Its control panel will open like this:

2. Click in the *Owner Name* box and type your name. Your first name's enough, unless someone else has the same name. In that case, use your first and last name or last initial.

3. Click in the *Owner Password* box and type a password. This can be up to eight characters long, and it should be easy to remember but hard to guess. If you think you might forget it, write it down some place where you can find it. Once you click away from the password box or close the window, the word you type is replaced by bullets so nobody can read it.

4. Click in the *Macintosh Name* box and type a name for your Mac. This can be something simple like Joe's Mac (assuming your name is Joe), or something unusual like the name of a city. It's a good idea to pick a descriptive name, something people will associate with you, since your Mac name is how other people will locate your files on the network. (See *Connecting your Mac to other* Macs on p. 173 below.)

If you're planning to start file sharing right away, don't close the Sharing Setup control panel. Instead, continue with the next section.

Turning file sharing on

To start file sharing, use the Sharing Setup control panel. Remember that when you turn file sharing on, it uses an extra 200K of your Mac's memory.

1. Open the Sharing Setup control panel if you haven't already. **Note:** you can't start file sharing without entering a *Macintosh name* and an *Owner name* (see above).

2. Click the *Start* button in the **File Sharing** area. The button name will change to *Cancel*, and the **Status** area will say that file sharing is starting up. Once it has, the *Cancel* button will change to *Stop*, and the Status area will say that file sharing is on.

3. Close the Sharing Setup control panel.

Now you're ready to identify specific folders or disks to share.

Sharing folders and disks

Whenever you create a new item, you are its owner, and only you can change the way it's shared, or its access privileges. You can share a single folder, several folders or an entire disk. To share individual files, put them in a folder and then share the folder. This way you can exchange information with others on your network without giving them access to files you want to keep private.

To share a folder:

1. Select the folder on the desktop.

2. Choose *Sharing...* from the File menu. (**Note:** if you don't have file sharing turned on or haven't selected a folder or disk, the *Sharing...* command is dimmed.) The sharing window for that folder appears, like this:

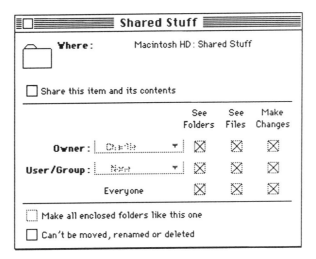

The window has the same name as the folder—each shared folder or disk can have its own sharing options. *Where* tells you the location of the folder.

3. Check the *Share this item and its contents* checkbox. The access privileges options become active in the middle part of the window (see Chapter 12, p. 186 for how to set them).

4. Close the window. This folder is now available for sharing.

A shared disk or folder icon looks like this:

(The icon name may be different in your case, but this distinctive icon tells you the item is shared over the network, rather than connected locally to your Mac.)

This is the quickest way to set up a folder or disk for sharing, but it makes the shared items available to everyone on your network. Following the above steps, you're letting others use a shared folder or disk as if it were their own. They can open, copy, rename or delete files or folders inside the shared item, just as you can. If you've shared your whole hard disk, they can even move, delete or rename shared folders on it.

Giving everyone on your network unlimited access to a shared item isn't necessarily a problem. On the other hand, you may want to restrict access to a shared item to a few specific users on your network, give different users different access privileges or prevent others from moving, deleting or renaming a shared folder. For more about controlling access by other users, see Chapter 12.

Monitoring shared folders

Whenever you're sharing files, you can find out who's using folders on your disk and, if you want, disconnect them.

1. Open the **File Sharing Monitor** control panel in the Control Panels folder. It looks like this:

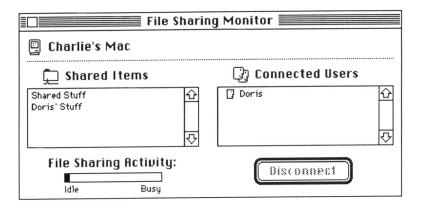

The **Shared Items** list shows the names of folders or disks you have made available for sharing from your Mac. The **Connected Users** list shows people who are currently sharing one or more of those folders (although it doesn't show which items each user is sharing).

Maximizing file-sharing performance

Whenever someone else on the network is sharing a file on your disk, your Mac has to spend some of its processing power handling that task. When several other people are sharing your files, this power drain can slow your own work down.

If the files being shared are small, you can fix this problem by asking other users to copy the files they need to their own disks. Then they can work with files on their own Macs and your Mac won't be involved in processing their work. (This will speed up the other users' work as well as yours—you always get better performance by working with a file on your own disk than with one over a network.) After the other users have made their changes to the shared files, they can save them back to your disk.

This solution works best with small files, which can be copied quickly over the network. Also, you may want to monitor what files are copied and when they're copied—especially if they're ones that several users share on a regular basis. If two users need to use the same file at the same time, and they both make changes to different copies of it, you'll have to reconstruct a single up-to-date file from the two modified versions—which can be difficult, if not impossible.

Disconnecting users

If you're backing up your hard disk, using a hard disk optimizer, working with sensitive information in a shared folder or performing other delicate operations, you may want to disconnect users currently sharing files with your Mac. In some cases you might want to disconnect just one user; in others, everyone—and it's unlikely you'll want to take the drastic step of turning off your Mac or disconnecting it from the network to accomplish this.

So, to disconnect one user:

1. Open the File Sharing Monitor control panel.

2. Select the name of the user you want to disconnect in the Connected Users list.

3. Click the **Disconnect** button. When you tell the Mac to disconnect a user, it displays a dialog box like this:

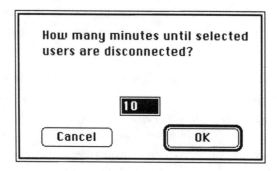

The default time is ten minutes, but you can set if for any amount (up to 999). To disconnect a user immediately, type [O] (zero).

4. Click the *OK* button. On the Mac you've just disconnected, a message will appear on its screen telling the user that he or she will be disconnected after the time you specified. When the

disconnection actually happens, the user will see another alert saying that he or she is no longer connected.

To disconnect everyone from your Mac at once:

1. Open the Sharing Setup control panel.
2. Click the *Stop* button in the File Sharing area. You'll see the above dialog box, for setting the time until disconnection.
3. Type in how much time you want to give them.
4. Click the *OK* button. Your Mac will stop sharing files when the time you set elapses.

Be careful when disconnecting users from your Mac. If other users are accessing files on your Mac when the disconnection occurs, it could damage your files. Even if you give people what seems like plenty of time to close any shared files, make sure they actually close them. A user with an open shared file might be out to lunch, for example, and not see your message until well after the disconnection and any damage has occurred. It's always a good idea to check verbally with connected users, if possible, to make sure they see the disconnect warning. (See Chapter 13 for more file sharing tips.)

Connecting your Mac to other Macs

So far, we've been covering making *your* Mac's files available for other Macs to share. When you want to connect to shared files on other Macs, the procedure's entirely different. You don't even need to have file sharing on.

Connecting to a shared item

To access a shared disk or folder on another Mac, you must connect (or log on) to the remote Mac you want to access, and then select the disk or folder you want to use. You use the AppleShare resource in the *Chooser* to do this:

1. Select the *Chooser* from the Menu. The Chooser window opens.

2. Click the AppleShare icon. At the right side of the window, a list of Macs available for sharing will appear, like this:

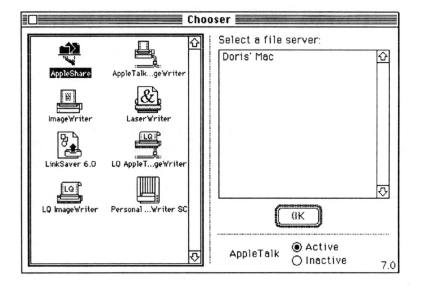

3. Select the name of the Mac you want to use and click the *OK* button. A **log-on** dialog box will appear, like this:

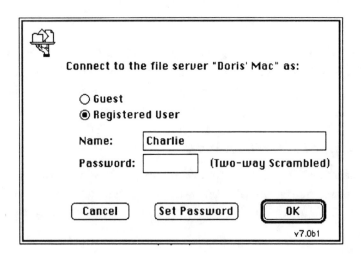

4. Your Mac's Owner name will appear in the *Name* box. If you aren't the Mac's owner, type your user name. Then press [Tab] and type your password. If you aren't a registered user for the Mac you want, click the *Guest* button to register as a guest. (If you don't know whether you have a registered user name, check with the other Mac's owner.)

5. Click *OK*. You'll be connected to the other Mac, and you'll see this dialog box for selecting specific shared items:

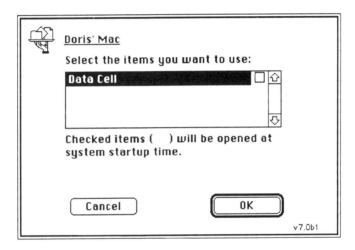

Only disks or folders that the remote Mac's owner has made available for sharing will appear in this dialog box.

6. Click on the folder or disk name you want to share. [Shift]-click or drag in the list to select more than one item.

7. Click *OK*. The shared item(s) will appear on your desktop.

Connecting to a shared item automatically at startup

If you use a shared item constantly, you may want to set up your Mac so it automatically puts the item on your desktop every time you start up. To do this:

1. Select all the items you want to share (steps 1 through 6 in the section directly above).

2. Check the checkbox(es) next to the item(s) you want automatically placed on your desktop. Two new buttons will appear at the bottom of the box, like this:

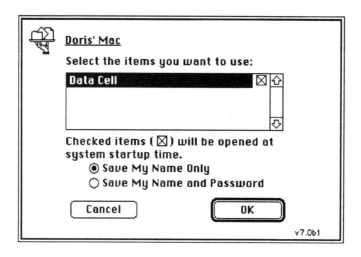

If you click the *Save My Name Only* button, then you'll be asked to enter your password each time your Mac starts up, (unless you've connected to the Mac as a guest user). If you're a registered user, choose this option when other people use your Mac and you don't want them to use the shared folders you've set to automatically be put on the desktop. When they start up your Mac, they won't know the password for the log-in dialog box, and they'll click the *Cancel* button. Then the Mac will start up, but the shared folder won't appear on the desktop.

If you click the *Save My Name and Password* button, then you'll automatically be logged on and the shared item will appear on your desktop without your having to do anything.

3. Click the *OK* button. The shared item will appear on your desktop, and it will appear there each time you start up your Mac.

Changing your password

If you're not using registered user names and passwords when you share files, skip this section.

When you share the files of several different Macs on your network, you must register and log on to each Mac individually. If you connect as a registered user rather than as a guest, it's best to use the same user name and password throughout. Otherwise, you'll have to remember which name and password you need for each Mac on your network.

Likewise, Mac owners must register users by name, so you should get together with others on your network to make sure you're all using the same names to register each other (see *File sharing tips* Chapter 13, p. 197). If they're not consistent, each file-sharing Mac's owner can change them so they are (owners can also allow for you to change your own password when they register your user name—see *Setting user access options*, Chapter 12, p. 182).

If you're allowed to change your password, you use the log-in procedure to do it; and in order to do it, you must know the existing one. (Otherwise, anyone could set the password and gain access to your files.) This is how you change it:

1. If you're already connected to the Mac where you want to change your password, disconnect from it by dragging the shared item's icon to the Trash on your desktop.

2. Select the file-sharing Mac you want with the *Chooser* (see *Connecting to a shared item*, p. 173 above if you need the steps). The log-in dialog box will appear.

3. Click the **Set Password** button. A dialog box will ask you to enter your current password and new password, like this:

4. Type your old password and new password in the boxes provided, then click *OK*. You'll be asked to reenter the new password to confirm it.

5. Re-enter your password and click *OK* again. The second dialog box appears so you can select specific shared items on the remote Mac's disk. From here, you can continue the log-in procedure normally.

Using a shared item

Once a shared item appears on your desktop, what you can do with it depends on the access privileges you have for that item. If an item has been shared following only the procedures in this chapter, it has the default access privileges and you'll be able to use the files in that item just as if they were on a disk connected locally to your Mac. But your access privileges for shared items may be restricted—see Chapter 12, p. 186.

If you have full access privileges within a shared folder or disk, you can make new folders inside it. As you know, when you make a new folder and become the folder's owner, only you can change that folder's access privileges. However, the remote Mac's owner is still the owner of the shared item that *contains* the folder you've created.

Disconnecting from a shared item

When you shut down your Mac, you'll be automatically disconnected from any shared items on your desktop. To disconnect from a shared item without shutting down:

1. Make sure you've closed all the files from the shared item.

2. Select the item's icon on the desktop and either drag it to the Trash, or choose *Put Away* from the File menu.

SHARING FILES AND LINKING PROGRAMS

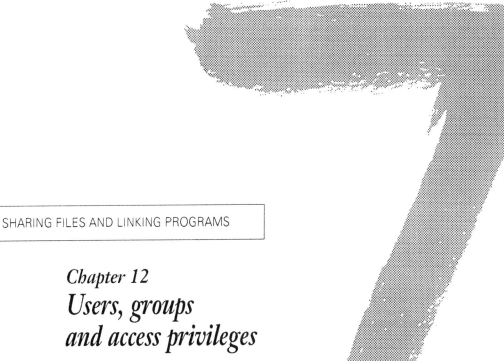

Chapter 12
Users, groups and access privileges

About users and groups **180**
About access privileges **186**
Viewing access privileges **189**
Access privileges in action **193**

As explained in Chapter 11, you can share your folders or disks with other users on a network. If you accept the default settings, sharing an item means that everyone on the network can see, copy, rename, change or delete the files in that item.

By registering **users** and **groups** and setting **access privileges**, though, you can specify who shares your files and what they can do with them:

- With registered users or groups, you can share items with some users but not with others.

- By changing access privileges, you control what others can do with your shared items. For example, you can let some users change the contents of a shared folder while letting others see the contents, but not change them.

In this chapter, we'll cover all the details of registering users and groups and setting access privileges. We assume you've read Chapter 11 or at least have registered your Macintosh name and owner name with the Sharing Setup control panel. If you haven't, see *Setting up file sharing* in Chapter 11, p. 166.

About users and groups

Registering users

As a Mac's **owner**, you control who can connect to your shared items. You register specific user names and then assign different access privileges to different users and to guests. Privileges for a particular user apply only to that user, while those you assign for guests apply to anyone who registers as a guest.

Before you can assign access privileges to a particular user, you must register that user's name. Register as many users as you want, as long as each of them has a unique name.

To register a user:

1. Open the **Users & Groups** control panel in the Control Panels folder. It looks like this:

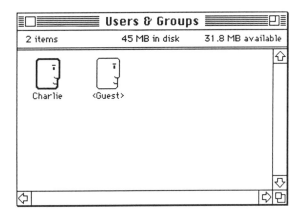

If the Users & Groups control panel hasn't been used on your Mac before, you'll only see two icons, one for a guest user and one for yourself as the Mac's owner. The owner's icon has a heavier outline, to distinguish it from other user icons.

1. Choose *New User* from the File menu. A New User icon appears in the control panel with the name selected, like this:

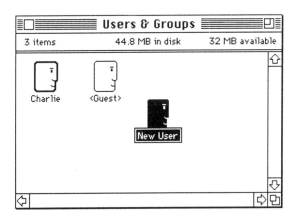

2. Type the user's name, and then press [Return] or [Enter], or click away from the icon to confirm the name change.

Setting user access options

Once you've created a user, you can set that user's **access options**. Access options determine the level of access a user may have to your shared items (subject to further restriction by the access privileges you set for each of those items; see p. 186). To set a user's access options:

1. Doubleclick that user's icon in the Users & Groups control panel. The user's window opens, like this:

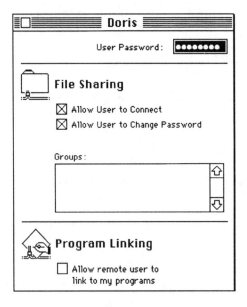

2. If you like, type a password the user will need to get into your system in the *User Password* box; then click away from the box. A string of bullets will replace the actual password to hide it from view. (It's usually better to let users select their own passwords; if you don't, be sure to tell them what their passwords are.)

The *Allow User to Connect* checkbox is normally checked so the user can connect to your Mac. Uncheck the box if you don't want the user to have access to your Mac.

The *Allow User to Change Password* checkbox is also normally checked, so the user can change the password you've entered. If you don't want the user to be able to change the password, uncheck the box.

The *Groups* list shows the names of all the groups to which the user belongs. At first this list will be blank because you haven't created any groups yet. (See *Registering groups*, p. 184 below).

Finally, the **Program Linking** area has a checkbox that lets a remote user's programs exchange information with programs on your disk. See Chapter 14 for more information on program linking.

Changing owner and guest access options

You can also set access options that always apply to guest users or to yourself as the Mac's owner (for times when you access this Mac from other Macs on the network).

To set the owner access options, doubleclick the owner's icon in the Users & Groups control panel. The owner window will appear, like this:

```
┌─────────────── Charlie ───────────────┐
│                                        │
│              User Password: ••••••••  │
│  ─────────────────────────────────────│
│   📁  File Sharing                     │
│                                        │
│       ☒ Allow User to Connect          │
│       ☒ Allow User to Change Password  │
│       ☒ Allow User to See Entire Volume│
│                                        │
│       Groups:                          │
│       ┌────────────────────────┐ ⇧    │
│       │                        │       │
│       │                        │       │
│       └────────────────────────┘ ⇩    │
│  ─────────────────────────────────────│
│   🏠  Program Linking                  │
│                                        │
│       ☐ Allow remote user to           │
│         link to my programs            │
└────────────────────────────────────────┘
```

The only difference between this window and an ordinary user window is the *Allow User to See Entire Volume* checkbox. Checking this allows you to access all the disks, folders or files on your Mac from another one, whether or not items have been shared—which is convenient if you have to use someone else's Mac.

To set guest options, doubleclick on the Guest icon in the Users & Groups control panel. The Guest window appears, like this:

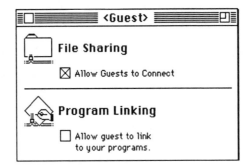

The only file sharing option here is to allow or deny guests access to your Mac. The default setting allows access. Uncheck the box if you don't want guests to connect to your Mac. (For more on the Program Linking option, see Chapter 14.)

Registering groups

Creating groups lets you assign the same access privileges to several users at the same time. Once you create a group, adding or removing users is easy.

To create a group of users:

1. Choose *New Group* from the File menu. A New Group icon appears in the Users & Groups control panel with the name selected, like this:

12. USERS, GROUPS AND ACCESS PRIVILEGES

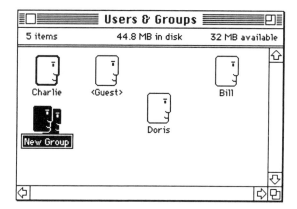

2. Type a different name for the group if you want, then press [Return] or [Enter] to confirm it, or click away from the icon.

3. To add users to the group, drag their icons on top of the new group icon. A message will tell you the user is being added to the group. But the user's icon still appears by itself in the Users & Groups control panel. (That's because a single user might have additional privileges beyond those assigned to any group he or she is part of.)

To see all the users in a group, doubleclick its icon. You'll see the group's window, like this:

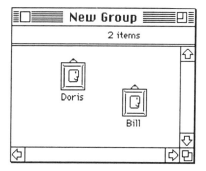

You can also add users to a group by dragging them inside this window.

Deleting users and groups

You can delete registered users or groups at any time. But you can't delete the Owner or Guest icons.

To **delete a user** from your Mac, select the user's icon in the Users & Groups control panel and drag it to the Trash.

To **delete a user from a group**, open the group window and drag the user's icon from there into the Trash. (This won't delete the user's icon from the Users & Groups control panel.)

To **delete an entire group**, select the group's icon in the Users & Groups control panel and drag it to the Trash. (This doesn't delete individual users from the Users & Groups control panel, only the group.)

About Access Privileges

Whether or not you register specific users on your Mac, you can specify access privileges for your shared items. (These may be items on your own hard disk, or ones you've created on another user's shared disk.)

Every time you select an item to share on your disk and choose the *Sharing...* command from the File menu, the sharing window presents you with several options for setting access privileges, defaulted like this:

As the shared item's owner, you can check the ***Share this item and its contents*** checkbox and the access privileges options in the middle of the window will become active. If you're not the owner, you can't share the item.

Kinds of access privileges

There are three classes of access privileges:

- ***See Folders*** means users can see a folder but not open it to see what's in it, or to work with its contents.

- ***See Files*** means users can open a folder and open its files or copy them to their own disks.

- ***Make Changes*** by itself means users can save new files to a folder. If *See Folders* and *See Files* are also checked, users can open the folder and open, copy, rename, change or delete files or folders within it.

You can use the checkboxes in any combination for different situations. When a box is checked, that privilege is granted; when it's unchecked, that privilege is withheld.

The sample window, Shared Stuff, on the preceding page shows the default access privileges. Everything is checked, so anyone who shares this item can do anything with it. For some examples of different access privileges you can set, see *Access privileges in action* at the end of this chapter, p. 193.

Classes of users

The sharing window lets you set access privileges for three levels of user: the Mac's **Owner**, a specific user or group of users (**User/Group**) and all other users (**Everyone**).

The Owner and User/Group boxes are actually pop-up menus. You can choose a new owner for the shared item or assign access privileges to a specific user or group by selecting different names from these pop-up menus. (Until you've registered other users and groups, the Owner menu will list only your name and *<Any User>*, and the User/Group menu will say *None*.)

If you're the owner of a folder, you want to be able to do anything with its contents, so you would normally leave all the *Owner* checkboxes checked. To restrict access privileges for specific users, groups or guests, uncheck the box(es) for the class(es) of privileges you want to deny.

Other access options

The two checkboxes at the bottom of the sharing window give you additional control over folder access.

The **Make all enclosed folders like this one** checkbox lets you copy the privileges of the current folder to any other folders contained in it—although you can give each folder its own access privileges, if you prefer. If you don't check this box or set specific privileges separately, any nested folders will have the default access privileges.

When you first make a new folder inside a shared disk or folder, its default access privileges are the same as the ones set for the disk or folder itself, and you're the new folder's owner.

The ***Can't be moved, renamed or deleted*** checkbox locks the folder so its name and location can't be changed. It's often a wise precaution, since you've probably given folders their names and locations for a good reason.

Using consistent user names

Once you register a user name, that user must use that exact name to connect to your Mac, so be sure to tell other users **exactly** what name you've registered them with.

So again, it's easiest if every Mac owner on the network uses the same set of names when registering users.

Viewing access privileges

With lots of people setting access privileges and sharing files, it's not always easy to remember which user has which privileges for each shared item, or even who owns each shared folder. Fortunately, there are lots of ways to find these things out.

Checking access privileges

To see the specific access privileges for an item and find out who owns it, use the *Sharing...* command on the File menu in the Finder:

1. Select the shared item.

2. Choose *Sharing...* from the File menu. The item's sharing window will open. If the shared item is one from your own disk and you're the item's owner, the access privileges options will be active. If the shared item you select is one you've connected to over the network, you'll see a sharing window like this:

```
┌─────────────────────────────────────────────┐
│ ▤□▤▤▤▤▤▤▤▤▤▤  Data Cell  ▤▤▤▤▤▤▤▤▤▤        │
│  ┌──┐                                       │
│  │📁│  Where:      Data Cell, Doris' Mac    │
│  └──┘                                       │
│        Connected As: Charlie                │
│        Privileges:   See Folders, See Files, Make Changes │
│  ─────────────────────────────────────────  │
│                         See    See    Make  │
│                       Folders  Files Changes│
│                                             │
│        Owner: [Doris    ]  ☒    ☒    ☒     │
│                                             │
│    User/Group: [Charlie ]  ☒    ☒    ☒     │
│                                             │
│              Everyone      ☒    ☒    ☒     │
│                                             │
│  ☐ Make all enclosed folders like this one  │
│                                             │
└─────────────────────────────────────────────┘
```

The sharing window for an item located on another Mac shows **Where** the item is located, the user name you've used to connect to that Mac (**Connected As**), and the access **Privileges** you have for that item. Notice that the Where information includes the disk name and Mac name. (If the Mac were on a different network zone, the zone name would follow the Mac name.)

Because you're not the item's owner, you don't have the option to share this item; all the access privilege options in the middle and bottom of the window are dimmed, because you aren't allowed to change them.

Folder privileges icons

Along with the *Sharing...* command, there are graphic clues to your access privileges with shared items. These are visible when you view folders and windows inside shared items on the desktop.

When you view a shared item by Icon, icons representing shared folders can be *plain, tabbed, belted* or *belted with an arrow.*

A **plain folder** icon looks just like any folder you've created on your own disk, and it means you can at least open the folder. (You'll need to select the folder and open it or choose *Sharing...* to see what privileges you may have beyond that.)

A **tabbed folder** looks like this:

Biz Research

When you have file sharing on, any folder on your disk that is available for others to share has a tabbed icon and network cables coming out of the bottom of it. When you view folders you own on other users' shared Macs, they also have a tabbed icon, but no network cables.

A **belted folder** looks like this:

Biz Research

This icon means this folder is off limits—you can't open it and don't have any privileges with it. Folders like this appear gray in list view windows.

There's also a **belted folder with an arrow**, like this:

Collection Box

This icon means you can't open the folder, but the arrow means you can save items to it. This type of folder is sometimes called a "drop box" because you can put things into it but you can't see its contents. With a folder like this, you have Make Changes privileges only.

Window privileges icons

When you open a shared folder or disk, its window may contain icons that tell you which access privileges you *don't* have. These icons appear at the left edge of the space just below the window's title bar, like this:

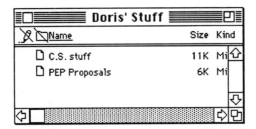

(This happens to be a list view window, but the icons show up in icon views as well.) In this case the user has See Files privileges, but not Make Changes or See Folders privileges—the pencil icon means *no changes* and the folder icon means *can't see folders*. (There are actually folders stored in this window's folder, but they're not visible because the user doesn't have privileges to see them.)

Along with the *no changes* and *can't see folders* icons, there's a *can't see files* icon like this:

If you had See Folders privileges only, you'd see this icon and the *no changes* one below the window's title bar. If you had full privileges, you wouldn't see any icons. In other words, the window shows you only what you can't do, not what you can.

Access privileges in action

The checkboxes in the sharing window allow you to assign many different combinations of privileges, but it isn't obvious how some of these combinations work. Here are some examples:

See Folders	See Files	Make Changes
☒	☒	☐

Here people can open files and folders inside the shared item and copy files to their own disks, but they can't add any new files or folders to it, and they can't change any of the existing items.

See Folders	See Files	Make Changes
☐	☒	☒

With this set of privileges, users can see individual files inside your shared item and make changes to them (or add new files or folders), but any folders inside the shared item will be invisible. This combination is good when you have private folders inside a shared item, because other users won't even be able to see them.

See Folders	See Files	Make Changes
☒	☐	☒

Here others can save new items to the shared item or to folders inside it, but they can't see any individual files in the shared item.

See Folders	See Files	Make Changes
☐	☒	☐

This option means others can't see folders inside the shared item or make any changes to it. They can only view, open and copy individual files inside the shared item.

```
    See    See   Make
  Folders  Files Changes
    ☐      ☐     ☒
```

This is the "drop box" option, with which others can save files into the shared item, but they can't open it to see its contents.

When you share files, there are lots of ways to set users, groups and access privileges to create a custom data security scheme on your Mac. As you experiment with these options, you'll find just the right combination of privileges, users and groups to give others exactly as much access to your files as they need.

SHARING FILES AND LINKING PROGRAMS

Chapter 13
File sharing tips and troubleshooting

File sharing tips **196**

File sharing troubleshooting **197**

File sharing can make you a lot more productive, but it's also fairly complex. In this chapter, we'll look at some ways to make file sharing as easy and reliable as possible and see how to solve some common problems.

File sharing tips

Some of these suggestions have been mentioned in Chapters 11 and 12, but this section expands on them.

Keep it simple

The more you use the various access privileges and user registration options available with file sharing, the more difficult it becomes to keep track of all the safeguards you've created. If you share files a lot, users will invariably want access to something on your Mac they can't get to, and you'll be forever resetting access privileges or moving files around. Eventually you may find just the right set of options for everyone, but it will take a while.

The best security system is the simplest. When you first turn on file sharing, there are no registered users (except yourself) and no groups of users. When you first share any item, everyone on the network has access to it. Unless you have a really good reason to limit access, don't do it, because you'll probably end up having to change it later. After all, you can limit access to files without setting special privileges or registering users or groups—just don't share them.

Use consistent user names and passwords

To access shared files on a Mac, a user must know the specific name and password under which he or she is registered on that particular Mac.

If you and others on your network are registering users, be sure you all use the same user names on every Mac. If a user is named Margaret, for example, don't register her as Margaret on one Mac, Maggie on another and Marge on a third. If you do, Margaret will have to remember how she's registered on every Mac.

What's good for user names is also good for passwords, only in this case it's best to let the user choose a password. When you create a new user, you have the option of entering a password for the user in the user window. Whether you enter a password or not, leave on the default setting in the user window which allows the user to change the password. (See *Changing your password* Chapter 11, p. 177.)

Use aliases

If you must frequently add users, create groups or monitor user activity on your Mac, create aliases for the Users & Groups and File Sharing Monitor control panels and put them on the menu. That way you don't have to open the Control Panels folder first to get to them. (See *The Make Alias command* in Chapter 5, p. 66, for more information.)

Save files locally

If a file-sharing Mac crashes while you're accessing its files, you'll lose your access to those files. If you're allowed to, save any shared file to your own hard disk as soon as you connect to the shared Mac. The file will then be safely stored on your disk in case the connection is broken.

Before shutting down or restarting a file-sharing Mac, choose one of the options to disconnect other users so they'll be warned. (See *Disconnecting users* and *Disconnecting from a shared item* in Chapter 11, p. 172 and p. 178 respectively.)

File sharing troubleshooting

Until you've used file sharing for a while, you may not know exactly what's gone wrong when something you don't expect happens. In this section, we'll take a quick look at some common file sharing problems.

File sharing won't start

If you can't start file sharing when you click *Start* in the Sharing Setup control panel, make sure you:

- are physically connected to an AppleTalk network
- have AppleTalk set to *Active* in the Chooser window
- have entered an Owner Name and Macintosh Name in the Sharing Setup dialog box

See *Turning file sharing on* in Chapter 11, p. 168 for more information.

You can't find a file-sharing Mac on the network

If you click on the AppleShare resource in the Chooser to display all the file-sharing Macs available and you don't see the Mac name you're looking for, there are a couple of possibilities:

1. The shared Mac doesn't have file sharing on. Check that Mac to see if this is the case.

2. Your Mac or the file-sharing Mac is physically disconnected from the network. To find out if this is the problem, click the LaserWriter resource in the Chooser window—from both your own Mac and the file-sharing one. If one or more LaserWriter names appear, then that Mac's connected to the network. (Remember, if your LaserWriter is turned off, it won't show up in the Chooser window.) If no names appear, check that the networking cable is plugged into your Mac's printer port or the network adapter card (if you have one).

If everything looks okay, you'll have to call a technician or your network administrator to diagnose the problem.

You can find a file-sharing Mac, but you can't connect to it

If you can see the file-sharing Mac you want but you have trouble connecting to it, there are two possible problems. Either you're using a name or password different from the one that's registered on that Mac, or the Mac's owner isn't allowing anyone to connect.

In either case, you'll see an alert box like this:

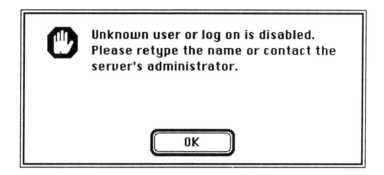

First try to enter your name and password a few times—you may have mistyped them. Make sure you're using uppercase or lowercase letters exactly as you're supposed to, and that you're not typing any extra spaces.

If this doesn't work, check your user name and password with the remote Mac's owner to make sure you're typing exactly the same ones registered on that Mac. You'll either correct your mistake or you'll find out that the Mac's owner isn't currently allowing people to connect.

You have forgotten your password

If you've forgotten your password, you have three remedies.

1. If another Mac owner set your password, ask him or her for it.

2. If the other Mac's owner set your password originally and doesn't remember it, he or she can enter a new one.

3. If you have physical access to the other Mac, you can use its Users & Groups control panel to re-register yourself.

The moral here is: *Don't forget your password*. Write it down some place where you can find it later.

You can connect to a file-sharing Mac, but you can't find the folder or disk you're looking for

In this case, the owner of the file-sharing Mac simply hasn't made the folder or disk available for sharing, or available to you. Check with the Mac's owner.

You can't change the access privileges for a shared item

This means you're not the item's owner. Look in the Owner box in the Sharing window to see who the owner is, then ask the owner to reset the privileges if you need more access (or reset them yourself at that owner's Mac, if it's available to you). If you want to control the access privileges, you'll have to get the owner to transfer the item's ownership to you.

You can't open a shared folder, see its files or save files to it

If you can connect to a shared folder but then can't open it on your desktop, see folders or files inside it, or save new or changed files to it, you don't have the necessary access privileges. Check with the owner of the folder to see if he or she will change the privileges for you. You can tell who owns the folder by selecting it on the desktop and choosing the *Sharing...* command from the File menu.

Sometimes you won't be aware that your privileges are limited until you try to save a document to a shared item. If you get an alert box that says you don't have the proper access privileges, check with the remote Mac's owner.

You can't move, rename or delete a shared item

In this case, the shared item's owner has created these restrictions by clicking the *Can't be moved, renamed or deleted* checkbox at the bottom of the folder's sharing window. To remove the restrictions, the folder's owner must select the item, choose *Sharing...* from the File menu, and uncheck the checkbox.

You can't find a user or group name

If you're trying to choose a name from one of the pop-up menus in the Sharing window and the user or group name doesn't appear, that user or group hasn't been registered on the Mac you're using. Even if you've registered users or groups on your own Mac, it doesn't mean that they are registered on other Macs. Each Mac owner must register the users or groups that will be allowed to connect to his or her Mac.

Your connection with a shared item is suddenly cut off

Your connection with a shared item may be deliberately cut off by the item's owner or accidentally disconnected by a system crash or network failure.

If the shared item's owner is cutting you off deliberately, you'll usually get a warning on your screen, like this:

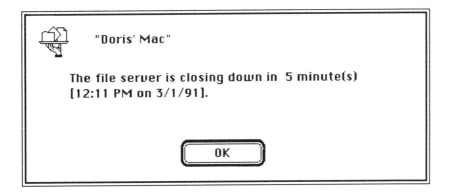

(You won't get warned in advance if the owner just shuts down or unplugs the Mac from the network.)

At the top of the box you'll see the name and location of the Mac that you're being disconnected from. A series of warnings like this means that you're being deliberately cut off. Ask the shared Mac's owner about reconnecting. To stop the messages from popping up, drag the shared item's icon to the Trash.

When a cutoff takes place, deliberate or not, you'll usually see an alert like this:

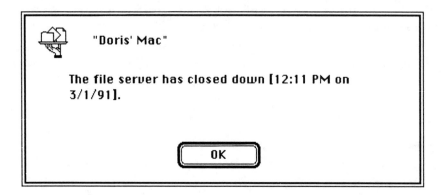

Check with the remote Mac's owner to see what went wrong. If the network's physical connection is broken, you may also see the above warning.

Sometimes, the double arrow icon will appear at the left edge of the menu bar to show that your Mac is using the network, but the arrows will stay there and your Mac will lock up. In this case you'll have to restart your Mac to continue working. This problem usually happens because of a physical disconnection on the network. Test your connection using step 2 in *You can't find a file-sharing Mac on the network* on p. 198.

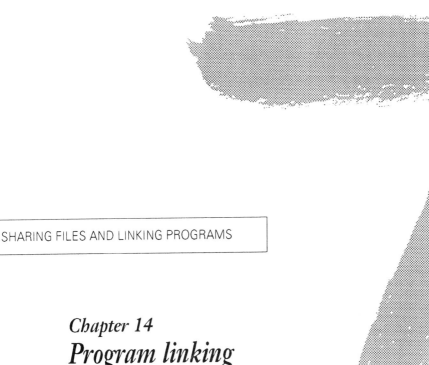

SHARING FILES AND LINKING PROGRAMS

Chapter 14
Program linking

Two ways to link programs **204**

Starting program linking **205**

Sharing your programs with other users **206**

Controlling other users' access to your shared programs **207**

Turning program linking off **208**

Managing program linking performance **209**

Program linking will let one program exchange information with another—on your Mac or across a network—without your intervention. For example, a word processing program on your Mac might send its text directly to a report created with your Mac's page layout program, or a spreadsheet on someone else's Mac might send its numbers to your Mac's business charting program.

System 7 makes program linking possible, but your programs must support linking before you can actually use it. It's like a telephone system: System 7 provides the basic telephone wires between different programs and lets you turn on the connections, but the individual programs must be able to understand each other once the connection is made.

If your applications support program linking, they'll have menu commands to control it and their manuals will explain how to use it. But before you can, you must turn program linking on using System 7. In this chapter, we'll look at how the new system software lets you activate and manage program linking.

Two ways to link programs

As with file sharing, there are different procedures for linking programs, depending on whether you or another network user is doing the linking.

1. **Linking from your Mac to other programs** If you're linking from a program on your Mac to programs on your Mac or on other networked Macs, you don't need to start program linking. Instead, you choose a command inside your program and then select the other program(s) you want to link to. This is managed entirely by individual programs, which will have their own specific menus, commands and dialog boxes. Check your program's manual for further instructions.

If you're linking to a program on a remote Mac, you'll have to connect to that Mac first, of course, either as a guest or with a registered user name (see *Connecting your Mac to other Macs*, Chapter 11, p. 173 for more information). And you'll only be able to link to those programs made available for that purpose (see *Controlling other users' access to your shared programs*, p. 207 below).

2. **Sharing your programs so others can link to them** If you're sharing your Mac's programs so other users on the network can link to them, you have to turn on program linking at your Mac and then identify the programs you want to share. There are various ways to control other users' access to your programs once you turn program linking on.

Starting program linking

Before you can even turn program linking on, you must be connected to an AppleTalk network and have AppleTalk set to *Active* in the Chooser window. If you're sharing a LaserWriter on a network, these have already been done. If you're connecting to a network for the first time, see *Setting up file sharing*, Chapter 11, p. 166, for network information.

Once you've got an AppleTalk network connected and active, you turn on program linking using the Sharing Setup control panel in the Control Panels folder. (That control panel is covered in detail in Chapter 11, p. 167.)

1. Open the Sharing Setup control panel.
2. Click the **Start** button in the **Program Linking** area at the bottom of the control panel.

    You'll see a message in the **Status** area that says program linking is starting up, and the *Start* button name will change to

Cancel. To cancel the startup at this point, click the *Cancel* button. Once program linking is on, the Status area will say so, and the *Cancel* button's name will change to *Stop*.

3. Close the Sharing Setup control panel.

Program linking is now on.

Sharing your programs with other users

Just as with shared items in file sharing, you must select specific programs you want to share for program linking, and then make them available to the network. (This isn't necessary if you're linking to other programs on your own Mac.) As with file sharing, you identify programs to share with the *Sharing...* command.

1. Choose a program you want to share by selecting its icon on the desktop.

2. Choose *Sharing...* from the File menu. The program's sharing window appears, like this:

3. Check the *Allow remote program linking* checkbox. If this box is dimmed, the program you've selected doesn't support program linking.

4. Close the sharing window. The program is now available for other users to link to.

Controlling other users' access to your shared programs

Other users who want to share your programs must first connect to your Mac, either as guests or as registered users with passwords. (See *Connecting your Mac to other Macs*, Chapter 11, p. 173, for more information.)

By granting access to specific users, as outlined in Chapter 12, you control who can link to your programs. By granting access to guest users, you can let anyone on your network link to your programs. Users and guests are not allowed program linking until you specifically permit it, which you do with the Users & Groups control panel:

1. Open the Users & Groups control panel in the Control Panels folder.

2. Doubleclick on the icon for the user whose access you want to change. The user's window opens, like this:

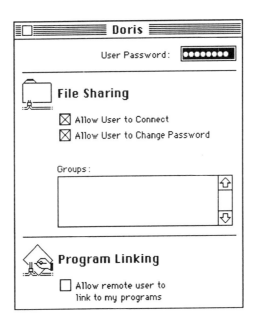

3. Check the *Allow remote user to link to my programs* checkbox in the Program Linking area.

4. Close the window.

That user can now link to your shared programs.

To stop a user from linking to your programs, uncheck the *Allow remote user...* checkbox. Unlike turning program linking off (see section below), this won't cut the user off if he or she is currently linked to programs on your Mac— but it will deny future access to that user.

Controlling access to guest users is just the same, except the checkbox in the Guest user's window says *Allow guest to link to my programs*.

Here's a review of the various access options you have with program linking and how to set them:

Access level	Action
No access to any program	Turn program linking off.
No access to a particular program	Don't share that program.
No access for a particular user No access for guests	For each user and guest, no access is the default, so just leave it alone.

Turning program linking off

When you want to stop program linking, just open the Sharing Setup control panel and click the *Stop* button in the Program Linking section of the window. Any users linked to that program will get an alert message that tells them the link has been broken.

Managing program linking performance

Whenever someone else's linked program is exchanging information with yours, it affects the performance of your Mac. Your Mac has to divide its resources between handling program linking and handling any work you're doing yourself. Apple says you can have up to 100 users linking to programs on your Mac at the same time, but it recommends no more than 50 users linked at a time.

The only way to regulate your Mac's performance with program linking is to limit the number of users who can link to your programs. The 50-user suggestion is an arbitrary one—with a Mac SE or another relatively low-powered machine, your Mac's performance will probably slow to an absolute crawl well before 50 users are linked.

Performance will also depend on which programs are linked, how much information they're exchanging and how often they exchange information. As always, experiment in your own situation to find out what suits you best.

Glossary

As you work with System 7, you'll run into unfamiliar terms and concepts dealing with new Macintosh capabilities. Most of these are defined the first time they appear in each chapter, but you can also look them up here for quick reference.

? menu

See *Help menu* below.

access options

In *file sharing*, a set of permissions assigned to a user which governs that user's basic abilities to connect to a shared Macintosh.

access privileges

The right to view or change specified files and/or folders in a shared folder or disk, given to other users on a *network*.

alias

A small file that represents and operates like another file, folder, disk—even the Trash. Aliases allow you to open these items from various places—like the menu, the Finder desktop or inside a folder.

AppleShare

1. Software that turns a Macintosh with a hard disk into a *file server*, and allows individual Macs on a *network* to share the files on that server.

2. A Chooser resource that lets you connect to other Macintoshes or AppleShare *file servers* on a *network*.

Apple Menu Items folder

A folder inside the System Folder that stores desk accessories or other items you want to appear on the menu.

Application menu

A menu in the Finder that displays all the programs or *desk accessories* *(DAs)* you currently have open.

Balloon Help

A feature in the Finder that automatically displays balloons containing explanations of different items, such as menus, commands or window elements, when you point to them with the mouse.

bit

The smallest possible unit of information. It can represent only one of two things: yes or no, on or off or—as it's expressed in the binary numbers used in computers—0 or 1. Short for *b*inary dig*it*. Also see *byte*.

bitmap

A pattern of dots used by the Mac's screen or a printer to represent a character or other graphic object.

byte

Eight *bits*. Bytes are typically used to represent characters (letters, numbers, punctuation marks and other symbols) in text.

cdev

A *control panel* device—in System 7, these are just called *control panels* (see below).

control panel

1. A program that lets you adjust an aspect of the Macintosh's operating characteristics (like its speaker volume, desktop pattern or networking features).

2. The dialog box you see when you open a control panel.

Control Panels folder

The folder inside the System Folder that stores *control panel* programs.

DA (desk accessory)

Programs available from the Finder *and* from within most applications, via the menu.

default

What you get if you don't specify something different. Often used to refer to standard settings (for example, the standard margins in a word processing program).

desktop

1. The Finder screen, showing the disks you currently have available for use with your Macintosh, the Trash icon and any files or folders you've moved out of their disk or folder windows.

2. A new organizational level at the top of the Mac's file storage system that shows any available disks or other items on the Finder desktop.

3. A button in the Open and Save dialog boxes of applications that lets you view all the disks or other items on the desktop.

Desktop Folder

An invisible folder, containing the files and folders stored on the Finder's desktop, that is automatically created on every disk by System 7. (If you restart under System 6, the folder becomes visible, and you have to open it to see the files and folders you'd had on the desktop under System 7.)

directory

An invisible file that keeps track of where various files are stored on a disk.

directory dialog box

A generic name for the dialog boxes you use to open or save files from within applications. Also known as a standard file box.

directory path

The path you must navigate through various folders to move from one organizational level to another in the Mac's file storage system.

download

To transfer a font file from a hard disk to a laser printer.

edition

A file containing data that you have selected from a document and made available for use in other documents under System 7's new Publish and Subscribe feature. Also see *publishing* and *subscribing*.

extension

A file that expands the Mac's system software capabilities, either by allowing it to communicate with other devices (such as printers, *file servers* or CD-ROM drives) or adding new functions like a menu bar clock. Files called *inits* or drivers under System 6 and previous system software versions are now called extensions.

Extensions folder

A folder inside the System Folder that contains *extension* files.

file server

A computer on a *network* that others on the *network* can access for applications and documents.

file sharing

The capability of networked Macintoshes to share the contents of folders with each other.

File Sharing Monitor

A *control panel* program that shows you which of your folders you have chosen to share with other users on a *network*, as well as which users are currently sharing those folders.

fixed-size font

A font that's only one point size, such as Geneva 14. Compare *outline* and *scalable* fonts.

Fkey program

A program that assigns a combination of [Shift], [⌘] and one of the number keys in the top row of the Mac keyboard to perform the same function at all times, no matter which program you have running.

gigabyte

A measure of computer memory, disk space and the like that's equal to 1024 *megabytes* (1,073,741,824 bytes), or about 179 million words. Sometimes a gigabyte is treated as an even billion *bytes* but, as you can see, that's almost 74 million *bytes* short. Sometimes abbreviated gig (more often in speech than in writing). Compare *kilobyte* and *megabyte*.

group

A collection of users on a *network* who have the same access to a designated shared folder or folders.

guest

In *file sharing*, someone who logs on to a *shared item*, but not as a *registered user*, and therefore gets the same *access privileges* assigned to all *guests*.

Help menu

A menu in the Finder that lets you turn on an automatic help function or display a list of keyboard shortcuts.

init

A program that loads automatically during the Mac's startup sequence, and which tells the System file to do something it wouldn't normally do, like recognize special keystroke sequences as commands. Under System 7, inits are now called *extensions*.

item

A generic name for any object that can be represented by an icon in the Finder: a disk, file, folder or the Trash.

kilobyte

A measure of computer memory, disk space and the like that's equal to 1024 *bytes* or about 170 words. Abbreviated K. Compare *megabyte* and *gigabyte*.

label

A name you can attach to a file to help you identify it, or to sort files into specific groups in Finder windows. On color Macintosh systems, a label can also assign a certain color to a file's icon in the Finder.

Label menu

A menu in the Finder that allows you to assign one of seven different *labels* to a selected item.

logging on

In *file sharing*, the process by which someone gains access to a *shared item* on another Mac (usually by entering a *user name* and password).

megabyte

A measure of computer memory, disk space and the like that's equal to 1024K (1,048,576 characters) or about 175,000 words. Abbreviated MB or meg.

network

Two or more computers (and/or other computer related devices) connected to share information.

outline font

A font designed for use on a laser printer or imagesetter. Rather than being composed of separate dots like a *fixed-size font*, it's made up of an outline of the shape of each letter and can be scaled to any size without loss of quality. Also see *scalable font*.

outline view

An arrangement of file or folder names in the Name, Date, Size, Kind and Label views of Finder windows that shows the contents of open folders, indented below the folder that contains them.

owner

The person who created and controls access to a folder, or who manages the *file sharing* functions on a particular Mac, as opposed to people who are simply using a folder or a Mac temporarily.

PMMU chip

A Paged Memory Management Unit chip, which must be added to the Macintosh II model computer before it can use System 7's *virtual memory* feature.

pop-up menu

A menu linked to a window title or other object on the screen, which appears when you point to the object and click the mouse button (and, in some cases, hold down one or more keyboard keys). Because they are attached to windows, dialog boxes and other movable items, pop-up menus can appear anywhere on the screen, instead of only appearing in a menu bar.

PostScript®

Adobe Systems, Inc.'s page-description programming language, designed to handle text and graphics and their placement on the page.

PostScript® font

An *outline font* that's described with *PostScript®*.

Preferences folder

A folder inside the System Folder that holds files which store the current settings for the Finder views, *file sharing*'s *registered users*, *guests* and *groups* and other user-adjustable features of the system software.

print spooler

A program (like PrintMonitor) that allows you to print a document into a special folder on your disk and have it fed to the printer from that folder while you get on with other work.

printer driver

A file that allows a Macintosh to print documents on a particular type of printer, like the ImageWriter or LaserWriter. You can't use any printer unless its driver is in your System folder (in System 7, it must be in the *Extensions folder*).

program linking

In System 7, a new capability that allows different programs to exchange information directly, without user intervention.

publishing

Making data from one program available for use by other Macs on the same *network* (see *subscribing*).

rdev

Any resource file in the Chooser window, including *printer drivers*, *network* drivers and resources that allow the Mac to communicate with other devices like scanners.

registered user

In *file sharing*, a user who has been assigned an individual set of *access options* to another user's *shared items*.

scalable font

A font that can be made any size you indicate, as opposed to being only one fixed size (compare *fixed-size font*).

screen font

A *bitmapped* version of an *outline font*, used to represent the font on the computer's screen.

SCSI

Short for small computer system interface. It's an industry-standard interface for hard disks and other devices that lets them transfer information very quickly. SCSI ports have been standard on all Macs since the Plus.

shared item

In *file sharing*, an item on a Mac which has been made available for others to use from their Macs on the same *network*.

startup disk

The disk you use to start up your Macintosh. This disk must contain a System Folder and the right system software files to start your Mac properly.

startup item

A file or program that is opened automatically when the Macintosh starts up.

Startup Items folder

A folder inside the System Folder that holds programs or documents that will be opened automatically when the Macintosh starts up.

stationery (stationery pad)

A document that stores text, graphics and/or formatting information and is opened automatically as an Untitled document whenever you doubleclick on it in the Finder or choose the *New* command in an application.

subscribing

Selecting published data made available from one location and pasting it into the current location, within or between documents—even between different applications or different computers on a network. Changes to the published data are automatically updated in the subscriber's copy of the data (see *publishing*).

suitcase (suitcase file, suitcase icon)

A file that contains one or more fonts or *desk accessories (DAs)*, so called because the icon representing this type of file looks like a suitcase.

32-bit addressing

Addressing is how the Mac organizes memory. The more addresses a Mac can handle, the more memory it can use. Macs that use 16-*bit* addressing can access as many different memory locations as can be specified by addresses that are 16 *bits* long. Some of the newer Macs can handle 32-*bit* addresses, which means the amount of memory they can address is much larger (up to 128 *megabytes* on some Macs).

Trash Folder

A System 7 folder containing files stored in the Trash. This folder is automatically created on every disk, and it's invisible if you start up your Mac with System 7. If you restart under System 6, the folder and any files in it are visible.

triangle (folder triangle)

An icon to the left of a folder icon in list view windows of the Finder, which you can click to show the folder's contents in *outline view* (or to hide them if they're already showing).

TrueType®

A new *scalable font* technology used with some fonts supplied with System 7. One TrueType file lets you print or display a given font clearly in any size.

user name

In *file sharing*, the name a *shared item*'s *owner* gives to a *registered user*.

Views

A *control panel* file that lets you change the way files and folders are shown in Finder windows.

virtual memory

The ability to set aside an unused portion of a hard disk as additional memory space for storing large programs or data files as you work with them on a Macintosh.

Index

Entries are only capitalized to indicate proper names (or other words that are always capitalized). They're alphabetized as if spaces did not exist: thus *Backgrounder* comes before *Background printing*. Numbers are alphabetized as if spelled out, according to the most common pronunciation. Page numbers in **boldface** indicate extended or important discussions.

A

About Balloon Help command, 86
About the Finder command, 41
About this Macintosh command, 41–42
accelerator cards and virtual memory, 124
Acceptance Delay buttons, 111
access privileges, **187–94**
    checkboxes, 186–89, 193–94
    classes of, 188
    classes of users, 188
    copying for enclosed folders, 188
    described, **186–89**
    drop boxes, 191, 194
    for guests, 184
    icons showing, 190–92
    locking folders, 189
    for owners, 183–84
    program linking, 207–08
    table of, 208
    tips, 196–97
    troubleshooting, 200
    user names, 189
    for users, 182–83
    using, **193–94**
    viewing, **189–92**
Access Privileges DA (defunct), 15, 21–22
active program, 87
Add button
    Download Fonts dialog box, 155
    Sound control panel, 114–15
alert boxes
    for overwriting files, 51
    PrintMonitor, 151
    for publishing and subscribing, 138
    sounds for, 113–14
Alert Sounds list, 114
aliases
    as menu items, 94–95, 105
    for control panels, 67, 68, 105
    described, 13
    file sharing users and groups, 196
    finding original file, 64
    getting information, 64–65
    illustrated, 66

aliases, *cont.*
    locking alias icons, 65
    making aliases, 66–67
    recognizing aliases, 67
    renaming, 67
    senseless aliases, 69
    as startup items, 38–39
    tips, 67–69
    troubleshooting, 69
    using aliases, 67–69
all at once checkbox, 73
Allow Guests to Connect checkbox, 184
Allow guest to link to my programs checkbox, 208
Allow remote program linking checkbox, 206
Allow remote user to link to my programs checkbox, 208
Allow User to Change Password checkbox, 183
Allow User to Connect checkbox, 183
Allow User to See Entire Volume checkbox, 184
Also display alert button, 153
Always snap to grid checkbox, 116–17
Apple CD-ROM init, 96
Apple HD SC Setup, 32
 menu
    (*also see* Apple Menu Items folder)
    About this Macintosh command, 41–42
    adding items
        aliases, 94–95, 105
        control panels, 105, 197

        DAs, 93–94
        documents, folders or programs, 94
        senseless additions, 95
    Apple Menu Items folder, **91–95**
    Chooser command, 44–45, 147–48, 166–67
    Control Panels command, 80, 95, 104
    illustrated, 92
    opening items from, 93
Apple Menu Items folder, **91–95**
    illustrated, 92
    installing items, 93–95
        aliases, 94–95
        DAs, 93–94
        documents, folders or programs, 94
    senseless items, 95
AppleShare
    eliminating old version, 21–22
    file sharing compared to, 162
    file sharing explained for AppleShare users, **162–64**
Apple system software files (*see* system software files)
AppleTalk
    eliminating old version, 21–22
    turning on, 166–67
AppleTalk ImageWriter file, 21–22
Application menu, 43, **86–88**
    activating a program, 87
    Hide command, 88
    Hide Others command, 88
    icon for, 86

INDEX

Application menu, *cont.*
    illustrated, 87
    Show All command, 88
applications *(see* programs)
automatic scrolling, 49
Available Fonts window, 156
    Delete button, 156

B

Backgrounder, 21–22
background printing, **44–45**, 147–48
Background Printing buttons, 45, 148
Balloon Help, 84–86
    illustrated, 85
Battery file, 21–22
Beep when modifier key is set checkbox, 112
belted folder icons, 190–91
bitmapped (fixed-size) fonts, 140, 142
Black & White button, 146
boldface convention in this book, 9
Brightness file, 21–22
bugs, 17
buttons
    Acceptance Delay buttons, 111
    Add button
        Download Fonts dialog box, 155
        Sound control panel, 114–15
    Also display alert button, 153
    Background Printing buttons, 45, 148
    Cancel Printing button, 150
    Cover Page buttons, 146
    Customize button, 25
    Desktop button, 128
    Destination buttons, 146–47
    Disconnect button, 172–73
    Download button, 156
    Download to buttons, 155
    Find button, 71
    Give no notification button, 153
    Initial Delay buttons, 111
    Maximum Speed buttons, 111
    More Choices button, 71–72, 74
    New Folder button, 129
    Only display ◆ in menu
        button, 153
    Options button
        Page Setup dialog box, 144
        Sound control panel, 114
    Pages buttons, 146
    Paper Source buttons, 146
    Pause button, 115
    Play button, 115
    Postpone indefinitely button, 151
    Print buttons, 146
    Record button, 115
    Remove button, 155
    Remove from List button, 150
    Save button, 157
    Save My Name and Password button, 176
    Save My Name Only button, 176

buttons, *cont.*
    Set Password button, 177
    Set Print Time button, 150–51
    Staggered grid button, 116
    Start button, 168, 205
    Stop button
        Sharing Setup control panel, 168, 173, 206, 208
        sound recording, 115
    Straight grid button, 116
    Switch Disk button, 24
by Color command (defunct), 77
by Label command, 77, 79

C

Calculate folder sizes checkbox, 118
Cancel Printing button, 150
Can't be moved renamed or deleted checkbox, 189
can't see files icon, 192
can't see folders icon, 192
Capture init, 96
CD-ROM disk
    installing System 7 from, 27, **28**
    loading installation files onto, 27
CE Software's DiskTop, 73
checkboxes
    access privileges checkboxes, 187–89, 193–94

all at once, 73
Allow Guests to Connect checkbox, 184
Allow guest to link to my programs checkbox, 208
Allow remote program linking checkbox, 206
Allow remote user to link to my programs checkbox, 208
Allow User to Change Password checkbox, 183
Allow User to Connect checkbox, 183
Allow User to See Entire Volume checkbox, 184
Always snap to grid checkbox, 116–17
Beep when modifier key is set checkbox, 112
Calculate folder sizes checkbox, 118
Can't be moved renamed or deleted checkbox, 189
Faster Bitmap Printing checkbox, 144
Flip Horizontal checkbox, 145
Font Substitution checkbox, 144
Graphics Smoothing checkbox, 144
Invert Image checkbox, 145
Larger Print Area checkbox, 145
Make all enclosed folders like this one checkbox, 190
Make Changes checkbox, 187
Precision Bitmap Alignment checkbox, 145
See Files checkbox, 187
See Folders checkbox, 187
shared item checkboxes, 176

checkboxes, *cont.*
    Share this item and its contents
        checkbox, 169, 187
    Show... checkboxes (Views control
        panel), 117–18
    Show disk info in header checkbox, 119
    Stationery pad checkbox, 131–32
    Text Smoothing checkbox, 144
    Unlimited Downloadable Fonts
        checkbox, 145
    Use key click sound checkbox, 111
    Use On/Off audio feedback checkbox, 110
    Warn before emptying, 84
checking, 9
Chooser command
    background printing, 44–45, 147–48
    connecting to shared items, 173–76
    turning on AppleTalk, 166–67
Chooser resources, 96
Chooser window, 44–45, 147–48
    Background Printing buttons, 45, 148
    illustrated, 45, 148, 167, 174
Clean Up commands, **81–82**
    Clean Up All, 57, 82
    Clean Up By Name, 57, 82
    Clean Up Desktop, 82
    Clean Up Window, 82
    invisible grid, 81–82
    Option with, 57, 82
Clipboard File, 21–22
Close command
    defunct, 60

PrintMonitor File menu, 151-52
CloseView control panel, 106
    eliminating old version, 21–22, 32
Close Window command, 60
    keyboard shortcut, 56
closing windows with keyboard shortcut, 58
Color control panel, **106–9**
    eliminating old version, 21–22
    Highlight color pop-up menu, 107
        Other command, 107–9
    illustrated, 107
    Window color pop-up menu, 107
Color/Grayscale button, 146
color picker dialog box, 108–9
colors
    for highlighted text, 106–9
    for icons, 45–46
    for labels, 45–46, 80
    for window borders, 106–7
color wheel, 108–9
commands
    (also see *specific menus and command*
        by name)
    keyboard shortcuts, 56–57
comments, finding files by, 71–73, 75
Connected Users list, 171
connecting
    to networks, 166
    to shared items, 173–75
        automatically at startup, 175–76
        disconnecting, 178

connecting, *cont.*
    passwords, 177–78, 199
    troubleshooting, 198–202
control panel file incompatibilities, 35
control panels, **104–20**
    (also see specific control panels by name)
    aliases, 67, 68, 197
    CloseView, 106
    Color, **106–9**
    defined, 9
    Easy Access, **109–12**
    eliminating old versions, 21–22
    File Sharing Monitor, 120, 170–71, 197
    General Controls, **112**
    Keyboard, **112–13**
    Labels, 119
    loading automatically at startup, 39
    Map, 106
    Memory, 120
    Monitors, 45, 106
    Mouse, 106
    pointer in, 106
    Sharing Setup, 120, 163, 167–68,
        171–73, 205–6, 208
    Sound, **113–15**
    Startup Disk, 37, 105, 106
    Users & Groups, 120, 181–86, 197, 207–8
    Views, **115–19**
Control Panels alias, 67, 95
Control Panels command, 95, 104
    Labels icon, 80
Control Panels folder, **95**, **104–5**
    illustrated, 104
    opening, 105
    opening control panels from, 105
    startup disk designation, 36–37
Copies option, 146
Copy command keyboard shortcut, 57
copying
    (also see moving*)*
    access privileges for enclosed folders, 188
    files, 50–51
    items, 58
    keyboard shortcut, 57
    system software floppy disks, 23
Cover Page buttons, 146
Create Publisher command, 135
Customize button, 25
customizing
    icons, 45–46, 61
    labels, **79–80**
    reinstalling custom system software
        files, 30–31
    System 7 installation, 25–26
    window layouts, 49
Cut command keyboard shortcut, 57

D

DA Handler, 21–22
DAL (Data Access Language), 15

DAs (desk accessories)
    alias uses, 68
    as menu items, 93–94
    loading automatically at startup, 39
    managing, 12
    preparing for System 7 installation, 21
    reinstalling in System Folder, 30–31
    removing from suitcase file, 93–94
    troubleshooting incompatibilities, 35
Data Access Language (DAL), 15
date created, finding files by, 71–73, 75
date modified, finding files by, 71–73, 75
Delete button, 156
deleting
    DAs from suitcase file, 93–94
    Desktop folder, 38
    emptying Trash, 51–52, 57, 83–84
    files, 51–52
    fonts from list to be downloaded, 155
    fonts from memory, disk or card, 156
    groups, 186
    startup items, 98
    Trash folder, 38
    TrueType fonts from LaserWriter disk, 158
    users, 186
desk accessories *(see* DAs)
desktop
    cleaning up, 57, 82
    desktop level, 127–29
    labeling items on, 79
    rebuilding desktop file, 58
Desktop button, 128

desktop file rebuilding, 58
Desktop folder, 38
desktop level, 127–29
Destination buttons, 146–47
dialog boxes
    (also see control panels; *specific dialog*
        boxes and control panels by name)
    color picker dialog box, 108–9
    for control panel programs, 9
    directory dialog box, 128, 129, 136
    Download Fonts dialog box, 154–56
    Easy Install dialog box, 24–26
    Find dialog box, **70–75**
    keyboard shortcuts, 56
    LaserWriter Options dialog box, 144–45
    log-on dialog box, 174–75
    Page Setup dialog box, 143–45
    Preferences dialog box, 152–53
    Print dialog box, 145–47
    Print Time dialog box, 150–51
    recording sounds, 114–15
    Set Password dialog box, 177–78
    for shared item selection, 175–76
    subscriber options dialog box, 137–38
directory dialog box
    Desktop button, 128
    Name of new edition entry box, 136
    New Folder button, 129
    for publishing and subscribing, 136
directory path pop-up window, 46, 58
Disconnect button, 172–73

disconnecting
  from shared items, 178
  shared item users, 163, 172–73
disk cache, 123–24
Disk First Aid, 32
disks *(see* floppy disks; hard disk)
DiskTop, 73
Display Available Fonts command, 156
documents
  (also see files; file sharing; programs;
    shared items)
  as menu items, 94
  getting information, 63–64
  loading automatically at startup, 39
  opening, 127–29
  publishing and subscribing, 14, **133–38**
  saving, 129
  stationery, 13, 64, **130–33**
dot-matrix printers
  background printing inoperable, 44
  printing with, **141–42**
downloadable fonts, 160
Download button, 156
Download Fonts command, 154–56
Download Fonts dialog box, 154–56
  Add button, 155
  Download button, 156
  Download to buttons, 155
  Fonts to download list, 155
  illustrated, 155
  Remove button, 155

downloading
  fonts, 154–56, 160
  PostScript fonts, 157–58
Download PostScript File command, 157–58
Download to buttons, 155
drop boxes, 191, 194
Duplicate command, 60
  keyboard shortcut, 56

E

Easy Access control panel, **109–12**
  eliminating old version, 21–22·
  illustrated, 109
  Mouse Keys, 110–11
  Slow Keys, 111
  Sticky Keys, 110, 111–12
  Use On/Off audio feedback checkbox, 110
Easy Install dialog box, 24–26
  Customize button, 25
  illustrated, 24
  Install button, 24
  Switch Disk button, 24
editions, 134
  (also see publishing and subscribing)
  naming, 136
Edit menu, **75**
  Create Publisher command, 135
  keyboard shortcuts, 57
  LaserWriter Font Utility Edit menu, 157

edit menu, *cont.*
    Subscriber options command, 137–38
    Subscribe to command, 136–37
Edit menu (LaserWriter Font Utility), 157
Eject command (defunct), 60
Eject Disk command, 60, 81
ejecting floppy disks, 52–53, 57
Empty Trash command, **83–84**
    (Option) with, 57, 83
    turning warning off, 57, 83–84
Erase Disk command, 81
erasing *(see* deleting)
error messages during installation, 29
extension files *(see* system extensions)
Extensions folder, **96**

F

Farallon Computing MacRecorder, 113, 114
Faster Bitmap Printing checkbox, 144
File Exchange, 32
File menu, **60–75**
    Close command (defunct), 60
    Close Window command, 60
    Duplicate command, 60
    Eject command (defunct), 60
    eliminated or moved commands, 60
    Find Again command, 70, **71**
    Find command, **70–75**
    Get Info command, 44, **61–65**, 131–33

Get Privileges command (defunct), 15, 60
keyboard shortcuts, 56
LaserWriter Font Utility File menu, **154–57**
Make Alias command, **66–69**
New Folder command, 60
New Group command, 185–86
New User command, 181–82
Open command, 60
Page Setup command, 60, 141, 143–45
Print command, 141, 145–47
Print Directory command (defunct), 60
PrintMonitor File menu, **151–53**
Print Window command, 60
Put Away command, 60, 178
renamed commands, 60
Save As command, 129
Save command, 129
Sharing command, 15, 66,
    169–70, 186–90, 206
unchanged commands, 60
File menu (LaserWriter Font Utility), **154–57**
    Display Available Fonts command, 156
    Download Fonts command, 154–56
    illustrated, 154
    Initialize Printer's Disk command, 156
    Page Setup command, 157
    Print Font Catalog command, 157
    Print Font Samples command, 157
File menu (PrintMonitor), **151–53**
    Close command, 152
    illustrated, 151
    Open command, 152

File menu (PrintMonitor), *cont.*
    Preferences command, 151, 152–53
    Resume Printing command, 152
    Stop Printing command, 152
files
    (*also see* documents; file sharing; programs; shared items; system software files)
    as menu items, 93–95
    copying, 50–51
    deleting, 51–52
    desktop file rebuilding, 58
    editions, 134
    file management changes, **49–52**
    finding
        again using same criterion, 71
        by name, 70–71, 74
        searching selected items, 73–74
        by size, kind or other criteria, 71–73, 74–75
        tips, 74–75
    getting information, 62–64
    init files, 96
    installing in System Folder, 91
    loading automatically at startup, 39
    locking programs, 63
    moving, 50–51
    opening, 49–50
    PostScript files, 145–46
    preference files, 97
    snapshot files, 53
    suitcase files, 93–94, 101–2
    System file, 20–22, **99–102**

file server
    installing System 7 from, **27–28**
    loading installation files onto, 27
file sharing, 13–14, **161–202**
    access privileges, **186–94**
        checkboxes, 187–89, 193–94
        classes of, 188
        classes of users, 188
        copying for enclosed folders, 189
        described, **186–89**
        drop boxes, 191, 194
        for guests, 184
        icons showing, 190–92
        locking folders, 189
        for owners, 183–84
        program linking, 207
        table of, 208
        tips, 196–97
        troubleshooting, 200
        user names, 189, 196–97
        for users, 182–83
        using, **193–94**
        viewing, **189–93**
    aliases, 197
    AppleShare compared to, 162
    for AppleShare users, **162–64**
        connecting to other file-sharing Macs, 163–64
        disconnecting users, 163
        monitoring users, 163
        sharing files with others, 163

file sharing, *cont.*
    connecting to other Macs, 163–64, **173–78**
        automatically at startup, 175–76
        connecting to a shared item, 173–75
        disconnecting from shared items, 178
        passwords, 177–78, 199
        troubleshooting, 198–202
        using shared items, 178
    described, 165
    disconnecting users, 163, 172–73
    drop boxes, 191, 194
    File Sharing Monitor control panel, 120, 170–73
        Connected Users list, 171
        Disconnect button, 172–73
        illustrated, 171
        Shared Items list, 171
    guests
        access privileges, 184–85
        icon for, 181
        program linking, 206–8
    icons, 181, 185
        for access privileges, 190–92
        for shared folders and disks, 170
    memory used by, 164
    monitoring shared folders, 163, 170–71
    performance control, 171–72
    program linking, 14–15, **204–9**
        to other programs, 204–5
        performance management, 209
        sharing your programs, 205, 206–8
        turning off, 208
        turning on, 205–6
    remote disk access signal, 164
    saving files, 197
    setting up, 166–68
        connecting to a network, 166
        identifying yourself and your Mac, 167–68
        turning on AppleTalk, 166–67
    Sharing command, 15, 66, 169–70
    sharing folders and disks, 169–70
    Sharing Setup control panel, 120
        File Sharing area, 168, 171–72, 173
        illustrated, 167
        Network Identity area, 168
    step-by-step, **164–73**
    tips, **196–97**
    troubleshooting, **197–202**
        access privileges can't be changed, 200
        connection cut off, 201–2
        disk can't be found, 200
        file-sharing Mac can't be connected to, 198–99
        file-sharing Mac can't be found, 198
        folder can't be accessed, 200
        folder can't be found, 200
        group can't be found, 201
        password forgotten, 199
        shared item can't be moved, renamed or deleted, 200
        startup doesn't work, 198
        user can't be found, 201
    turning on file sharing, 168

file sharing, *cont.*
   users and groups, **180–86**
      deleting users and groups, 186
      deleting users from groups, 186
      disconnecting users, 163, 172–73
      guest access privileges, 184
      owner access privileges, 183–84
      program linking, 206–9
      registering groups, 185–86
      registering users, 180–82, 189
      user access privileges, 182–83
      user names, 189, 196–97
File Sharing Monitor control panel, 120, 170–71
   alias for, 197
   Connected Users list, 171
   Disconnect button, 172–73
   illustrated, 171
   Shared Items list, 171
Find Again command, 70, **71**
   keyboard shortcut, 56
Find button, 71
Find command, **70–75**
   all at once option, 73
   finding again using same criterion, 71
   finding files by name, 70–71
   finding files by size, kind or other criteria, 71–73, 74–75
   Find within option, 72, 73
   keyboard shortcut, 56
   pop-up menus, 72–73
   searching selected items, 73–74
   tips, 74–75

Find dialog box, **70–75**
   all at once checkbox, 73
   Find button, 71
   Find within pop-up menu, 72, 73
   illustrated, 70, 72
   More Choices button, 71–72, 74
Finder, **41–58**
   (also see specific menus and commands by name)
   differences from Multifinder, 43
   ejecting floppy disks, 52–53
   eliminating old version, 20–22
   file management changes, **49–52**
      copying files, 50–51
      deleting files, 51–52
      moving files, 50–51
      opening files, 49–50
   FKeys, **52–53**
   icon cosmetics, **45–46**
   keyboard shortcuts, **54–58**
      dialog box shortcuts, 56
      Edit menu command shortcuts, 57
      File menu command shortcuts, 56
      Finder Shortcuts command, 86
      miscellaneous shortcuts, 58
      navigating folders or windows, 54–55
      selecting icons, 54
      Special menu command shortcuts, 57
   loading multiple programs, 43
   memory management, **43–44**
   new features, 12
   new menus and commands, 41–42

Finder, *cont.*
- printing in the background, **44–45**
- screen snapshots, 53
- selecting icon names, 42
- stationery creation in, 131–33
- window changes, **46–49**
  - automatic scrolling, 49
  - customizing window layouts, 49
  - list view window outline structure, 48
  - list view windows Label category, 47
  - pop-up window path, 46, 58
  - selecting groups of items, 49
  - zoom box operation, 47

Finder Shortcuts command, 86
Finder Startup, 21–22
Find within option, 72, 73
Find within pop-up menu, 72, 73
First Page button, 146
fixed-size fonts, 140, 142
FKey program incompatibilities, 35
FKeys, **52–53**
- ejecting floppy disks, 52–53
- screen snapshots, 53

Flip Horizontal checkbox, 145
floppy disks
- *(also see* hard disks)
- copying original disks, 23
- ejecting, 52–53, 57
- getting information, 65
- installing System 7 from, **23–26**
- showing info in list view window header, 119
- starting from, 34
- startup disk scanning order, 36

folders
- *(also see* file sharing; System Folder; *specific folders by name)*
- alias uses, 68
- as menu items, 94
- getting information, 65
- invisible folders, 38
- keyboard shortcuts for navigating, 54–55
- opening automatically at startup, 98
- shared folders
  - access control, 170
  - alias uses, 68–69
  - connecting to, 173–76
  - copying access privileges for enclosed folders, 189
  - disconnecting from, 178
  - drop boxes, 191, 194
  - icons, 170, 190–92
  - locking, 189
  - monitoring, 170–71
  - passwords, 177–78, 199
  - sharing, 169–70
  - troubleshooting, 200
  - using, 178
- sizes in list views, 118
- in Startup Items folder, 98

Font/DA Mover, 12, 15, 21–22, 32
Font for views pop-up menu, 116

fonts
> *(also see* printing)
> displaying available fonts, 156
> downloadable, 160
> downloading, 154–56, 160
> file formats, 101
> fixed-size (bitmapped) fonts, 140, 142
> installing in System file, **99–102**
> LaserWriter Font Utility, 32, **153–58**
> managing, 12
> PostScript fonts, 140–41
>> downloading, 157–58
>> mixing with TrueType fonts, 159
>> screen fonts for, 159
>
> preparing for System 7 installation, 21
> printing list of, 157
> printing samples of, 157
> reinstalling in System Folder, 30–31
> screen fonts, 140–41, 159
> TrueType fonts, 13, 100, 141
>> with ImageWriters, 142
>> mixing with others on LaserWriter, **159–60**
>> removing from LaserWriter disk, 158
>> viewing, 100
>
> types available, 140–41
> viewing, 100, 156

Fonts to download list, 155
Font Substitution checkbox, 144
Font Utility *(see* LaserWriter Font Utility)
foreign character sets, 112–13

G

General cdev (defunct), 21–22, 112
General Controls control panel, **112**
> eliminating old version, 21–22
> RAM cache options moved, 112

Get Info command, **61–65**
> alias information, 64–65
> customizing icons, 61
> disk information, 65
> document information, 63–64
> folder information, 65
> keyboard shortcut, 56
> memory management using, 44
> program information, 62–63
> Stationery pad checkbox, 131–32
> turning Trash warning off, 83–84

Get Privileges command (defunct), 15, 60
Give no notification button, 153
Graphics Smoothing checkbox, 144
gray shades
> for icons, 45–46
> printing, 146

groups, 185–86
> *(also see* file sharing; users)
> access privileges, **186–94**
> deleting, 186
> deleting users from, 186
> new group icon, 185
> registering, 185–86

Groups list, 183

group window
    illustrated, 185
    viewing users, 185
guests
    (also see file sharing; users)
    access privileges, 184, 208
    icon for, 181
    program linking, 206–8
Guest window
    Allow Guests to Connect checkbox, 185
    illustrated, 184

H

hard disk(s)
    (also see file server; floppy disks; shared items)
    alias uses, 69
    getting information, 65
    installing System 7 from, 27, **28**
    loading installation files onto, 27
    local vs. remote, 27
    not working properly, 29
    printer hard disk initialization, 156
    reclaiming disk space after installation, 32
    SCSI address for, 36
    shared disks
        access control, 170
        icon, 170
        sharing, 169–70

showing info in list view window header, 119
startup disk switching, 36–37
startup problems, 35
startup scanning order, 36
Help menu, 13, **84–86**
    About Balloon Help command, 86
    Balloon Help, 84–86
    Finder Shortcuts command, 86
    Hide Balloons command, 86
    Show Balloons command, 85
Hide Balloons command, 86
Hide command, 88
Hide Others command, 88
Highlight color pop-up menu, 107
highlight colors, 106–7

I

Icon and Small Icon Views options, 116–17
    Always snap to grid checkbox, 116–17
    Staggered grid button, 116
    Straight grid button, 116
icons
    (also see aliases)
    access privileges shown by, 190–92
    Application menu icons, 86
    cleaning up, 57
    colors and gray shades for, 45–46

icons, *cont.*
   customizing, 61
   file sharing, 170, 181, 185, 190–92
   folder privileges icons, 190–92
   guest icon, 181
   keyboard shortcuts for selecting, 54
   locking alias icons, 65
   new group icon, 185
   new user icon, 181
   Orientation icons, 144
   owner icon, 181
   selecting, 42
   selecting icon names, 42
   for shared folders and disks, 170
   stationery icon, 130
   Sticky Keys icon, 111
   Views control panel options, 116–17
   window privileges icons, 192
ImageWriter
   background printing inoperable, 44
   eliminating old driver, 21–22
   printing with, **141–42**
   restarting (initializing), 158
ImageWriter file, 21–22
init files, 96
Initial Delay buttons, 111
Initialize Printer's Disk command, 156
INITPicker, troubleshooting incompatibilities
     using, 35
inits (*see* system extensions)
Install button (Easy Install dialog box), 24
Installer program
   after the Installer is finished, 29–31
   missing or damaged files, 29
   necessity for, 20
   running from floppy disks, 23–24
installing
   (*also see* installing System 7)
   custom system software files, 30–31
   files in System Folder, 91
   fonts in System file, **99–102**
   items in Apple Menu Items folder, 93–95
     aliases, 94–95
     DAs, 93–94
     documents, folders or programs, 94
     senseless items, 95
   sounds in System file, **99–102**
   System 7, **20–32**
installing System 7, **20–32**
   after the Installer is finished, **29–31**
   best way, **20–22**
   from CD-ROM disk, 27, **28**
   Customize option, 25–26
   eliminating old System Folder, 20–22
   error messages, 29
   from file server, **27–28**
   from floppy disks, **23–26**
   Installer program necessity, 20
   from local hard disk, 27, **28**
   reclaiming disk space, **32**
   reinstalling custom system software
     files, 30–31
   replacing an old System Folder, **23**
   troubleshooting, **29**

Invert Image checkbox, 145
invisible folders, 38

K

keyboard
    click sound control, 111
    FKeys, **52–53**
    foreign character sets, 112–13
    shortcuts, **54–58**
    speed control, 111
    sticky keys (modifier key sequences) control, 111–12
    turning repeat on and off, 111
    using instead of mouse, 110–11
Keyboard control panel, **112–13**
    eliminating old version, 21–22
    illustrated, 113
    Keyboard Layout list, 113-14
Keyboard Layout list, 113-114
keyboard shortcuts, **54–58**
    dialog box shortcuts, 56
    Edit menu command shortcuts, 57
    File menu command shortcuts, 56
    Finder Shortcuts command, 86
    FKeys, **52–53**
    for folders, 54–55
    miscellaneous shortcuts, 58
    selecting icons, 54
    Special menu command shortcuts, 57
    for windows, 54–55, 58
Key Layout file, 21–22
kind, finding files by, 71–73, 74

L

Label category, 47, 78–79
    illustrated, 47, 78, 79
Label menu, **77–80**
    applying labels, 79
    colors on, 45–46, 80
    customizing labels, **79–80**
    illustrated, 78
    list views Label category and, 47
labels
    applying to desktop items, 79
    colors for, 45–46, 80
    finding files by, 71–73, 75
    renaming, 80
    sorting windows by, 79
Labels control panel, 119
Larger Print Area checkbox, 145
Laser Prep file, 21–22
LaserWriter
    background printing, 44–45
    eliminating old driver, 21–22
    hard disk initialization, 156
    mixing TrueType fonts with others on, **159–60**

LaserWriter, *cont.*
   printing with, **143–47**
   PrintMonitor, **147–53**
   restarting (initializing), 158
LaserWriter file, 21–22
LaserWriter Font Utility, **153–58**
   Edit menu, 157
   eliminating old version, 32
   File menu, **154–57**
      Display Available Fonts command, 156
      Download Fonts command, 154–56
      illustrated, 154
      Initialize Printer's Disk command, 156
      Page Setup command, 157
      Print Font Catalog command, 157
      Print Font Samples command, 157
   Utilities menu, **157–58**
      Download PostScript File command, 157–58
      illustrated, 157
      Remove TrueType command, 158
      Restart Printer command, 158
      Start Page Options command, 158
LaserWriter Options dialog box, 144–45
   Flip Horizontal checkbox, 145
   illustrated, 144
   Invert Image checkbox, 145
   Larger Print Area checkbox, 145
   Precision Bitmap Alignment checkbox, 145
   Unlimited Downloadable Fonts checkbox, 145
Last Page button, 146

linking programs *(see* program linking)
List Views options, 117–19
   Calculate folder sizes checkbox, 118
   Show... checkboxes, 117–18
   Show disk info in header checkbox, 119
list view windows
   Alert Sounds list, 114
   Connected Users list, 171
   disk information in, 119
   folder sizes in, 118
   Fonts to download list, 155
   Groups list, 183
   Keyboard Layout list, 112-13
   Label category, 47
   Microphones list, 114
   outline view, 48
   selecting groups of items, 49
   Shared Items list, 171
   Views control panel options, 117-19
   Waiting list, 150
loading
   (also see opening)
   files automatically at startup, 39
   installation files onto CD-ROM disk, hard disk or file server, 27
   multiple programs, 43
   preventing system extensions (inits) from loading, 34, 58
local hard disk *(see* hard disk)
locking
   alias icons, 65
   finding locked files, 71–73, 75

locking, *cont.*
    modifier key, 112
    programs, 63
    shared folders, 189
log-on dialog box, 174–75
    illustrated, 174
    Name box, 175
    Set Password button, 177
LQ AppleTalk ImageWriter file, 21–22
LQ ImageWriter file, 21–22

M

Macintosh Bible Guide to System 7, The
    conventions in, 9–10
    how to use, 9
    organization of, 8–9
    readers' skills assumed by, 7–8
    who the book is for, 7
Macintosh models, System 7 on, 16–17
Macintosh Name box, 168
MacRecorder, 113, 114
MacroMaker (defunct), 15, 21–22
Make Alias command, **66–69**
    making an alias, 66–67
    senseless aliases, 69
    tips, 67–69
    troubleshooting aliases, 69
    using aliases, 67–69

Make all enclosed folders like this one checkbox, 189
Make Changes checkbox, 187
Manual Feed button, 146
Map control panel, 106
    eliminating old version, 21–22
Maximum Speed buttons, 111
Memory control panel, 120, 122–27
    disk cache, 123–24
    illustrated, 123
    32-bit addressing, 126–27
    virtual memory, 124–26
memory (RAM)
    (also see virtual memory)
    addressing capabilities of Mac models, 16–17
    disk cache, 123–24
    file sharing usage, 164
    program memory management, **43–44**, 62–63, **122–27**
    disk cache, 123–24
    Memory control panel, 122–27
    resetting the current memory, 62–63, 122
    32-bit addressing, 126–27
    virtual memory, 124–26
System 7 requirement, 7
32-bit addressing, 14, 16–17, 126–27
virtual memory, 14, 16–17, 124–26

menus
    (also see pop-up menus; *specific menus and commands by name)*
     menu, 41–42, 44–45, 80, 92
    Application menu, 43, **86–88**
    Edit menu, 57, **75**
    Edit menu (LaserWriter Font Utility), 157
    File menu, 56, **60–75**
    File menu (LaserWriter Font Utility), **154–57**
    File menu (PrintMonitor), **151–53**
    Help menu, 13, **84–86**
    keyboard shortcuts, 56–57
    Label menu, **77–80**
    new menus and commands, 41–42
    Special menu, 57, **81–84**
    Utilities menu (LaserWriter Font Utility), **157–58**
    View menu, **77**
Microphones list, 114
modifier key, sticky keys settings, 111–12
Monitors control panel, 106
    displaying color or shades of gray, 45
    eliminating old version, 21–22
More Choices button, 71–72, 74
mouse, using keyboard instead, 110–11
Mouse control panel, 106
    eliminating old version, 21–22
Mouse Keys, 110–11
    Initial Delay buttons, 111
    Maximum Speed buttons, 111
moving
    (also see copying)

Desktop folder, 38
files, 50–51
Trash folder, 38
MultiFinder
    (also see Finder)
    elimination of, 12, 16, 21–22
    System 7 Finder differences, 43

N

Name box, 175
Name of new edition entry box, 136
names/naming
    (also see aliases)
    alias names, 67
    editions, 136
    finding files by name, 70–71, 74
    registering
        groups, 185–86
        users, 180–83, 189, 196–97
    renamed File menu commands, 60
    renaming labels, 80
    selecting icon names, 42
networking
    (also see file sharing; groups; program linking; users)
    connecting to a network, 166
    file sharing, 13–14, **161–202**
        access privileges, 182–85, **186–94**, 207–8

networking, *cont.*
    aliases, 197
    AppleShare compared to, 162
    for AppleShare users, **162–64**
    connecting automatically to a shared item at startup, 175–76
    connecting to a shared item, 173–75
    connecting to other Macs, 163–64, **173–78**, 198–202
    described, 165
    disconnecting from shared items, 178
    disconnecting users, 163, 172–73
    drop boxes, 191, 194
    File Sharing Monitor control panel, 120, 170–73
    guest access options, 184
    icons, 170, 181, 185, 190–92
    memory used by, 164
    monitoring shared folders, 163, 170–71
    owner access options, 183–84
    passwords, 177–78, 199
    performance control, 171–72
    program linking, 14–15, **204–9**
    remote disk access signal, 164
    setting up, 166–68
    Sharing command, 15, 66, 169–70
    sharing folders and disks, 169–70
    Sharing Setup control panel, 120, 167–68, 171–73
    step-by-step, **164–73**
    tips, **196–97**
    troubleshooting, **197–202**
    turning on file sharing, 168
    Users & Groups control panel, 120
    users and groups, **180–86**
    using shared items, 178
    program linking, 14–15, **204–9**
        to other programs, 204–5
        performance management, 209
        sharing your programs, 205, 206–8
        turning off, 208
        turning on, 205–6
    publishing and subscribing, 14, **133–38**
    System 6 and System 7 coexistence, 17–18
New Folder button, 129
New Folder command, 60
    keyboard shortcut, 56
New Group command, 185–86
New User command, 181–82
no changes icon, 192
numeric keypad, 110–11

O

Only display ◆ in menu button, 153
Open command, 60
    keyboard shortcut, 56
Open command (PrintMonitor File menu), 152
opening
    (also see loading)
    control panels, 105

opening, *cont.*
    Control Panels folder, 104
    documents, 127–29
    files, 49–50
    files automatically at startup, 39
    folders automatically at startup, 98
    items from menu, 93
    PrintMonitor window, 149
    screen snapshots with TeachText, 53
    stationery, 132, 133
    suitcase files, 101
    System file, 99
Options button
    Page Setup dialog box, 144
    Sound control panel, 114
Orientation icons, 144
Other command, 107–9
outline view, 48
    illustrated, 48
Owner Name box, 168
Owner Password box, 168
Owner pop-up menu, 188–89
owners
    (also see file sharing*)*
    access privileges for, 183–84
    changing, 188
    icon for, 181
owner window
    Allow User to See Entire Volume checkbox, 184
    illustrated, 183

P

Paged Memory Management Unit (PMMU) chips, 124
Pages buttons, 146
Page Setup command, 60, 141, 143–45
    LaserWriter Font Utility File menu, 157
Page Setup dialog box, 143–45
    Faster Bitmap Printing checkbox, 144
    Font Substitution checkbox, 144
    Graphics Smoothing checkbox, 144
    illustrated, 143, 144
    Options button, 144
    Orientation icons, 144
    Paper options, 143
    Printer Effects options, 144
    Reduce or Enlarge option, 143
    Tabloid pop-up menu, 143
    Text Smoothing checkbox, 144
Paper Cassette button, 146
Paper options, 143
Paper Source buttons, 146
passwords, 177–78, 199
Paste command keyboard shortcut, 57
Pause button, 115
performance *(see* speed*)*
Personal LaserWriter file, 21–22
PICT format screen snapshots, 53
Picture files, 53
plain folder icon, 191
Play button, 115

PMMU (Paged Memory Management Unit) chips, 124
pop-up menus
    desktop level on, 129
    directory path pop-up window, 46, 58
    Find command, 72–73
    Find within pop-up menu, 72, 73
    Font for views pop-up menu, 116
    Highlight color pop-up menu, 107
    Owner pop-up menu, 188–89
    Subscriber to pop-up menu, 138
    Tabloid pop-up menu, 143
    User/Group pop-up menu, 188–89
    Window color pop-up menu, 107
pop-up window path, 46, 58
    illustrated, 46
Postpone indefinitely button, 151
PostScript File button, 146–47
PostScript fonts, 140–41
    downloading, 157–58
    mixing with TrueType fonts, 159
    screen fonts for, 159
Precision Bitmap Alignment checkbox, 145
preference files, 97
Preferences command, 151, 152–53
Preferences dialog box, 152–53
    Show the PrintMonitor window when printing option, 152
    When a manual feed job starts options, 153
    When a printing error needs to be reported options, 152–53
Preferences folder, **97**

Print buttons, 146
Print command, 141, 145–47
    keyboard shortcut, 56
Print dialog box, 145–47
    Copies option, 146
    Cover Page buttons, 146
    Destination buttons, 146–47
    illustrated, 145
    Pages buttons, 146
    Paper Source buttons, 146
    Print buttons, 145
Print Directory command (defunct), 60
Printer button, 146
printer drivers
    eliminating old versions, 21–22
    networking with System 6-based and System 7-based Macs, 17–18
Printer Effects options, 144
printers
    (also see fonts)
    ImageWriter
        background printing inoperable, 44
        printing with, **141–42**
    LaserWriter
        background printing, 44–45
        hard disk initialization, 156
        mixing TrueType fonts with others on, **159–60**
        printing with, **143–47**
        PrintMonitor, **147–53**
    restarting (initializing), 158
Print Font Catalog command, 157

Print Font Samples command, 157
printing, **140–60**
   (also see fonts)
   background, **44–45**
   font formats for, 140–41
   font samples, 157
   fonts list, 157
   with ImageWriter, **141–42**
   with LaserWriter, **143–47**
   LaserWriter Font Utility, 32, **153–58**
   LaserWriter Options dialog box, 144–45
   Page Setup dialog box, 143–45
   Print dialog box, 145–47
   PrintMonitor, **147–53**
   startup page, 158
Printing box, 149
PrintMonitor, **147–53**
   alerts, 151
   eliminating old version, 21–22
   File menu, **151–53**
     Close command, 152
     illustrated, 151
     Open command, 152
     Preferences command, 152–53
     Resume Printing, 152
     Stop Printing command, 152
   PrintMonitor Documents folder
     creation by, 97
   PrintMonitor window, **149–51**
   starting, **147–48**
PrintMonitor Documents folder, **97**
PrintMonitor window, **149–51**

Cancel Printing button, 150
   illustrated, 149
   opening, 149
   Printing box, 150
   Remove from List button, 150
   Set Print Time button, 150–51
   Waiting list, 150
Print Time dialog box, 150–51
   illustrated, 151
   Postpone indefinitely button, 151
Print Window command, 60
program linking, 14–15, **204–9**
   to other programs, 204–5
   performance management, 209
   sharing your programs, 205, 206
     controlling users' access, 207–8
   turning off, 208
   turning on, 205–6
programs
   (also see documents; files; program linking)
   activating from Application menu, 87
   alias uses, 68
   as menu items, 94
   getting information, 62–63
   hiding and showing windows, 88
   identifying active program, 87
   linking, 14–15, **204–9**
   loading automatically at startup, 39
   loading multiple programs, 43
   locking, 63
   memory management for, **43–44**,
     62–63, **122–27**

programs, *cont.*
    disk cache, 123–24
    resetting the current memory, 62–63, 122
    32-bit addressing, 126–27
    virtual memory, 124–26
  version information, 62
publishing and subscribing, 14, **133–38**
  alert boxes for, 138
  described, 134
  directory dialog boxes for, 136
  editions, 134
  options, 137–38
  using, 135–37
Put Away command, 60, 178
  keyboard shortcut, 56

Reduce or Enlarge option, 143
registering
  groups for shared items, 185–86
  users of shared items, 180–83, 189, 196–97
remote hard disk *(see* file server)
Remove button, 155
Remove from List button, 150
Remove TrueType command, 158
removing *(see* deleting)
renaming *(see* names/naming)
resources, snd, 101
Responder, 21–22
Restart command, 81
Restart Printer command, 158
Resume Printing command, 152

Q

QuickMail init, 96

R

RAM *(see* memory)
RAM cache (disk cache), 123–24
rebuilding desktop file, 58
Record button, 115

S

Save As command, 129
Save As dialog box, 130–31
Save button, 157
Save command, 129
Save dialog box, 129
Save My Name and Password button, 176
Save My Name Only button, 176
· saving
  documents, 129
  PostScript files, 145–46

saving, *cont.*
    shared files, 197
    stationery, 133
Scrapbook File, 21–22
screen fonts, 140–41, 159
screen snapshots, 53
scrolling, automatic, 49
SCSI address and startup disk scanning order, 36
searching
    again using same criterion, 71
    for files by name, 70–71, 74
    for files by size, kind or other criteria, 71–73, 74–75
    selected items, 73–74
    tips, 74
security *(see* access privileges)
See Files checkbox, 187
See Folders checkbox, 187
Select All command keyboard shortcut, 57
selecting
    (also see searching)
    fonts to be downloaded, 155
    groups of items in list views, 49
    icon names, 42
    icons, 42
    icons with keyboard shortcuts, 54
    shared items, 175
Set Password button, 177
Set Password dialog box, 177–78
Set Print Time button, 150–51
Set Startup command (defunct), 16, 81, 98

    (also see Startup Items folder)
shared item checkboxes, 175
shared items
    access control, 170
    alias uses, 68–69
    connecting to, 173–76, 198–202
    disconnecting from, 178
    drop boxes, 191, 194
    icon, 170
    icons showing privileges, 190–92
    locking shared folders, 189
    monitoring, 170–71
    passwords, 177–78, 199
    sharing, 169–70
    sharing window for, 190
    troubleshooting, 200
    using, 178
shared items dialog box, 175–76
    Save My Name and Password button, 176
    Save My Name Only button, 176
Shared Items list, 171
Share this item and its contents checkbox, 169, 187
Sharing command, 15, 66
    checking access privileges, 189–90
    program linking, 206
    setting access privileges, 186–89
    sharing folders and disks, 169–70
sharing files *(see* file sharing)
Sharing Setup control panel, 120
    for AppleShare users, 163
    disconnecting everyone, 173

Sharing Setup control panel, *cont.*
    File Sharing area, 168
        slide control, 171–72
        Start button, 168
        Stop button, 168, 173
    identifying yourself and your Mac, 167–68
    illustrated, 167
    Network Identity area, 168
        Macintosh Name box, 168
        Owner Name box, 168
        Owner Password box, 168
    Program Linking area, 205–6
        Start button, 205
        Stop button, 205, 208
    turning on file sharing, 168
sharing window, 169–70, 186–89,
    189–90, 206
    Allow remote program linking
        checkbox, 206
    Can't be moved renamed or deleted
        checkbox, 189
    illustrated, 169, 187, 190, 206
    Make all enclosed folders like this one
        checkbox, 189
    Make Changes checkbox, 187
    Owner pop-up menu, 188–89
    program's sharing window, 206
    See Files checkbox, 187
    See Folders checkbox, 187
    shared item information in, 189–90
    Share this item and its contents
        checkbox, 169, 187

    User/Group pop-up menu, 188–89
shortcuts *(see* keyboard shortcuts)
Show All command, 88
Show Balloons command, 85
Show... checkboxes (Views control panel),
    117–18
Show disk info in header checkbox, 119
Show the PrintMonitor window when
    printing option, 152
Shut Down command, 81
size
    of current program memory, 62–63, 122
    of disk cache, 124
    finding files by, 71–73, 74–75
    folder sizes in list views, 118
    of virtual memory, 124–26
Slow Keys, 111
    Acceptance Delay buttons, 111
    Use key click sound checkbox, 111
snapshot files, 53
snd resources, 101
sorting windows by label, 79
Sound control panel, **113–15**
    Add button, 114–15
    Alert Sounds list, 114
    eliminating old version, 21–22
    illustrated, 114
    Microphones list, 114
    Options button, 114
    Speaker Volume control, 114

sounds
    for alerts, 113–14
    Easy Access siren, 110
    file formats, 101
    installing in System file, **99–102**
    key clicks, 111
    managing, 12
    microphone choices, 114
    modifier key beep, 112
    playing, 100
    preparing for System 7 installation, 21
    recording, 113, 114–15
    reinstalling in System Folder, 30–31
    snd resources, 53
    speaker volume control, 114
Speaker Volume control, 114
Special menu, **81–84**
    Clean Up commands, **81–82**
    Eject Disk command, 60, 81
    Empty Trash command, **83–84**
    Erase Disk command, 81
    keyboard shortcuts, 57
    Restart command, 81
    Set Startup command (defunct), 16, 81
    Shut Down command, 81
speed
    file sharing performance control, 171–72
    keyboard speed control, 111
    program linking performance management, 209
    virtual memory performance decrease, 124, 126

Staggered grid button, 116
Start button, 168, 205
starting *(see* startup; turning on)
Start Page Options command, 158
startup, **34–39**
    connecting to shared items automatically, 175–76
    disk scanning order, 36
    file sharing won't start, 198
    from floppy disks, 34
    loading files automatically, 38
    with more than one hard disk connected, 36–38
    preventing system extensions (inits) from loading, 34, 58
    PrintMonitor, **147–48**
    rebuilding desktop file, 58
    starting system extensions (inits), 96
    Startup Items folder, 16, 38–39, **98**
    switching startup disks, 36–37
    system software incompatibilities, 34–35
Startup Device file (defunct)
    (also see Startup Disk control panel)
    eliminating old version, 21–22
startup disk
    scanning order, 36
    switching disks, 36–37
Startup Disk control panel, 37, 105, 106
    illustrated, 37, 105
    pointer in, 106
startup items, 38
    aliases as, 38–39

startup items, *cont.*
  limit on, 98
  removing, 98
  system extensions (inits) vs., 98
Startup Items folder, 16, 38, **98**
  aliases in, 38–39
  folders in, 98
startup page, 158
stationery, 13, 64, **130–33**
  changing a stationery pad, 133
  icon, 130
  making in Save As dialog box, 130–31
  making in the Finder, 131–33
  opening, 132, 133
  saving, 133
Stationery pad checkbox, 131–32
Sticky Keys, 110, 111–12
  Beep when modifier key is set
    checkbox, 112
  icon, 111
  locking modifier key, 112
Stop button
  Sharing Setup control panel, 168, 173, 206, 208
  sound recording, 115
stopping *(see* turning off*)*
Stop Printing command, 152
Straight grid button, 116
StyleWriter
  (also see dot-matrix printers*)*
  background printing inoperable, 44
Subscriber options command, 137–38

subscriber options dialog box, 137–38
  Subscriber to pop-up menu, 138
Subscriber to pop-up menu, 138
Subscribe to command, 136–37
subscribing *(see* publishing and subscribing*)*
Suitcase
  elimination of need for, 12
  preparing for System 7 installation, 21
suitcase files
  installing DAs from, 93
  installing fonts from, 101–2
  opening, 101
  removing DAs from, 93–94
Switch Disk button, 24
system extensions (inits)
  Chooser resources, 96
  Extensions folder, **96**
  incompatibilities, **34–35**
  init files, 96
  preventing from loading, 34, 58
  reinstalling in System Folder, 30–31
  startup items vs., 98
System file, **99–102**
  changing, 101
  eliminating old version, 20–22
  fonts and sounds in
    file formats, 101
    installing, 102
    playing and viewing, 100
  illustrated, 99
  opening, 99

System Folder, **90–102**
   (also see specific system folders by name)
   Apple Menu Items folder, **91–95**
   Control Panels folder, 36–37, **95**
   eliminating old version, 20–22
   Extensions folder, **96**
   illustrated, 90
   installing files in, 91
   Preferences folder, **97**
   PrintMonitor Documents folder, **97**
   reinstalling custom system software files, 30–31
   Startup Items folder, 16, 38–39, **98**
   unblessing, 20–21
   why not to replace, 23

System 7
   bug possibilities of, 17
   control panels, **104–20**
   cost of, 7
   deciding to upgrade or not, **17–18**
   eliminated features, **15–16**
   file sharing, 13–14, **161–202**
   Finder, **41–58**
   hardware requirements for, 7, **16–17**
   incompatibilities with, **34–35**
   installing, **20–32**
   menus and commands, **60–88**
   new features, **12–15**
   printing, **44–45, 140–60**
   program linking, 14–15, **204–9**
   startup, **34–39**
   System Folder, **90–102**
   using applications, **122–38**
   version numbers on screen illustrations, 10

System 6
   features not in System 7, 15–16
   networking with System 7-based Macs, 17–18

system software files
   eliminating old versions, 21–22
   reinstalling custom files, 30–31
   running incompatibilities, 35
   startup incompatibilities, 34–35

T

tabbed folder icon, 191
TeachText
   eliminating old version, 21–22, 32
   opening screen snapshots with, 53
   stationery demonstration using, 130
Text Smoothing checkbox, 144
32-bit addressing, 14, 126–27
   Mac models capable of, 16–17, 126
   turning on, 127
32-bit QuickDraw file, 21–22
tips
   alias uses, 67–69
   file sharing, **196–97**
   finding files, 74–75
   virtual memory, 126

Trash
    alias uses, 69
    emptying, 51–52, 57, 83–84
    turning off warning when emptying,
        57, 83–84
Trash folder, 38
Trash information window
    illustrated, 84
    Warn before emptying checkbox, 84
troubleshooting
    aliases, 69
    file sharing, **197–202**
        access privileges can't be changed, 200
        connection cut off, 201–2
        disk can't be found, 200
        file-sharing Mac can't be connected
            to, 198–99
        file-sharing Mac can't be found, 198
        folder can't be accessed, 200
        folder can't be found, 200
        group can't be found, 201
        password forgotten, 199
        shared item can't be moved,
            renamed or deleted, 200
        startup doesn't work, 198
        user can't be found, 201
    startup problems, **34–35**
    System 7 installation failure, **29**
    system software incompatibilities, **34–35**
TrueType fonts, 13, 100, 141
    with ImageWriters, 142
    mixing with others on LaserWriter, **159–60**

    removing from LaserWriter disk, 158
    viewing, 100
turning off
    keyboard repeat, 111
    program linking, 208
    startup page, 158
    warning when emptying Trash, 57, 83–84
turning on
    AppleTalk, 166–67
    file sharing, 168
    keyboard repeat, 111
    program linking, 205–6
    startup page, 158
    32-bit addressing, 127

U

unchecking, 9
Undo command keyboard shortcut, 57
Unlimited Downloadable Fonts checkbox, 145
upgrading
    cost of, 17
    need for, 17–18
Use key click sound checkbox, 111
Use On/Off audio feedback checkbox, 110
User/Group pop-up menu, 188–89
User Password box, 182
Users & Groups control panel, 120
    alias for, 197

Users & Groups control panel, *cont.*
   deleting users and groups, 186
   guest access privileges settings, 184
   illustrated, 181, 185
   owner access privileges settings, 183–84
   program linking, 207–8
   registering groups, 185–86
   registering users, 181–82
   user access privileges settings, 182–83
users, **180–86**
   (also see file sharing; groups)
   access privileges, 182–83, **186–94**, 208
   classes of, 188–89
   deleting, 186
   disconnecting, 163, 172–73
   guests
      access privileges, 184
      icon for, 181
      program linking, 206–8
   new user icon, 181
   program linking, 206–9
   registering, 180–82, 189
user's window
   Allow guest to link to my
      programs checkbox, 208
   Allow remote user to link to my programs
      checkbox, 208
   Allow User to Change Password
      checkbox, 183
   Allow User to Connect checkbox, 183
   Groups list, 183
   illustrated, 182, 207
   Program Linking area, 183
   User Password box, 182
Utilities menu (LaserWriter Font
      Utility), **157–58**
   Download PostScript File command,
      157–58
   illustrated, 157
   Remove TrueType command, 158
   Restart Printer command, 158
   Start Page Options command, 158

V

version numbers on screen illustrations, 10
viewing
   (also see Get Info command)
   access privileges, **189–93**
   fonts, 100, 156
View menu, **77**
   by Color command (defunct), 77
   by Label command, 77, 79
Views control panel, **115–19**
   Font for views pop-up menu, 116
   Icon and Small Icon Views area, 116–17
      Always snap to grid checkbox, 116–17
      Staggered grid button, 116
      Straight grid button, 116
   illustrated, 116

virtual memory, 14, 124–26
   accelerator cards and, 124
   hardware required, 16–17, 124
   Mac models capable of, 16–17
   performance decrease from, 124
   setting, 124–26
   tips, 126
VM Storage file, 125–26
volume control, 114

owner window, 183–84
pop-up window path, 46, 58
PrintMonitor window, **149–51**
sharing window, 169–70, 187–89, 190–91, 206
sorting by label, 79
user's window, 182–83, 207–8
window privileges icons, 192
zooming improvement, 47

W

Waiting list, 150
Warn before emptying checkbox, 84
When a manual feed job starts options, 153
When a printing error needs to be reported options, 152–53
Window color pop-up menu, 107
windows, **46–49**
   (also see list view windows)
   automatic scrolling, 49
   Available Fonts window, 156
   cleaning up, 57, 82
   color for borders, 106–7
   customizing, 49
   group window, 184–85
   Guest window, 184
   hiding and showing, 88
   keyboard shortcuts, 54–55, 58

Z

zooming improvement, 47

Macintosh® Bible products

The Macintosh Bible, Third Edition. It's the best-selling Mac book ever, with 484,000 copies in print (including five foreign translations). The Third Edition has **1,115 pages**, with a 90-page index and a 68-page glossary. At 2½¢ a page for the best—and most clearly written—Mac information available, how can you go wrong? **$28.**

The Macintosh Bible Software Disks, Third Edition. This companion to *The Macintosh Bible* is full of great public-domain software, shareware, templates, fonts and art. Painstakingly gleaned from literally thousands of programs, these disks offer you *la crème de la crème*. Over 1.5 megabytes of software on two 800K disks. **$20.**

The Macintosh Bible "What Do I Do Now?" Book. This best-seller covers just about every basic problem a Mac user can encounter through System 6.0.7 (many tips and solutions are applicable to System 7 too)—from the wrong fonts appearing in a printout to the mouse not responding. Clear, straightforward and written by veteran Mac author Charles Rubin, it's an essential guide for beginners and experienced users alike. **$12.**

The Macintosh Bible Guide to System 7. System 7 represents the most dramatic changes ever made to the Mac's basic system software, and sets the stage for all future system improvements. Our crystal-clear, accessible and affordable guide, written by veteran Mac author Charles Rubin, gets you up to speed with System 7 in no time. **$12.**

The *Bible*/software combo. Save $10 when you buy *The Mac Bible* and the software together. **$38.**

The two-book combo. Save $5 by buying *The Mac Bible* and *"What Do I Do Now?"* together. **$35.**

The super combo. Save $12 when you buy *The Macintosh Bible*, the software disks and *The "What Do I Do Now?" Book* together. **$48.**

The ultra combo. Save $14 when you buy *The Macintosh Bible* with the software disks, *The "What Do I Do Now?" Book* and our *Guide to System 7*. **$58.**

The Macintosh Bible T-Shirt. Our T-shirts are striking—bright magenta lettering on your choice of black or white. Here's a little picture of the front. On the back they say: **Easy is hard** *(The second commandment from The Macintosh Bible).* These are high-quality, preshrunk, 100% cotton shirts; they're thick, well-made and run large. **$9.**

To order any of these products, just fill out the form on the next page, tear it out (it should come out cleanly and won't hurt the book) and send it with your payment to **Goldstein & Blair, Box 7635, Berkeley CA 94707.** (If the form is gone, don't despair; all the information you need to order is on this page.) You can also order by phone with Visa or MasterCard. Call us at 510/524-4000 between 10 and 5, Pacific Time, Mon–Fri (or leave your phone number on our answering machine). **All our products have a 30-day money-back guarantee.** If you're not *completely satisfied* with anything you order from us, just return it within 30 days, with your receipt, in resellable condition (i.e. not damaged) and get all your money back—cheerfully refunded, no questions asked—including what we charged to ship you your order *and* whatever you spent to return it to us (by UPS ground or parcel post).

Shipping **and handling to anywhere in the US costs $4, regardless of how much (or little) you order, and that includes tax (if any).** Our basic *non-US* rates cover shipment by air to Canada and Mexico and by surface to everywhere else; they're $3 per copy for the software disks or the T-shirt (T-shirts are shipped free when ordered with other products), $5 per *"What Do I Do Now?"* or *Guide to System 7*, $7 per *Macintosh Bible*, $10 per *Bible*/software, two-book or super combo, $12 per ultra combo. For shipment by air to countries other than the US, Mexico or Canada, consult the back side of the facing order form, or write or call. (Also call or write for shipping rates on orders of three or more items.)

Order form for Macintosh Bible products

Please send me:

_____ copies of *The Macintosh Bible, Third Edition*	@ $28 =	$_____
_____ copies of *The Macintosh Bible Software Disks, Third Edition*	@ $20 =	$_____
_____ copies of *The Macintosh Bible "What Do I Do Now?" Book*	@ $12 =	$_____
_____ copies of *The Macintosh Bible Guide to System 7*	@ $12 =	$_____
_____ copies of the *Bible*/software combination	@ $38 =	$_____
_____ copies of the two-book combo	@ $35 =	$_____
_____ copies of the super combo	@ $48 =	$_____
_____ copies of the ultra combo	@ $58 =	$_____
_____ *Macintosh Bible* T-shirts	@ $ 9 =	$_____

(in black:___S ___M ___L ___XL; in white:___S ___M ___L ___XL)

shipping, handling and tax (if any): $_____
[$4 total per order in the US; see facing page for other rates]

TOTAL: $_____

☐ I'm enclosing a check for the total shown above. *(Customers outside the US: checks must be in US funds and payable through a US bank. You can also pay with an international postal money order, but not a Eurocheque. It's easiest if you pay by credit card.)*

☐ Please charge my charge card for the total amount shown above:

VISA card #_____ exp. date _____

MasterCard #_____ exp. date _____

cardholder signature _____

Ship this order to: *(PLEASE PRINT CLEARLY)*

_____
name

_____
address (please give us a street address so we can ship via UPS)

_____
city/state/zip

_____
daytime phone number (with area code)

Enclose this order form with your payment in an envelope and send it to:
Goldstein & Blair, Box 7635, Berkeley CA 94707
Thanks.

Just tear this page out of the book. (It should come out cleanly and won't hurt the book.)

To order more Mac Bible products, use the form on the other side of this sheet.

International airmail shipping rates

These rates *only* apply to products shipped by *airmail* to countries other than the US, Canada & Mexico. *For all other shipping rates,* see the product information page facing the order form (two pages back).

Colombia, Venezuela, Central America and the Caribbean:

- $11 per *Macintosh Bible*
- $5 per T-shirt, software disks, *"What Do I Do Now?"* or *Guide to System 7*
- $15 per *Bible*/software, two-book or super combo
- $18 per ultra combo

South America (except Colombia & Venezuela), Europe (except the USSR), Morocco, Algeria, Libya, Egypt & Tunisia:

- $18 per *Macintosh Bible*
- $6 per T-shirt or software disks
- $8 per *"What Do I Do Now?"* or *Guide to System 7*
- $23 per *Bible*/software or two-book combo
- $25 per super combo
- $30 per ultra combo

Everywhere else:

- $24 per *Macintosh Bible*
- $8 per T-shirt or software disks
- $11 per *"What Do I Do Now?"* or *Guide to System 7*
- $31 per per *Bible*/software or two-book combo
- $35 per super combo
- $42 per ultra combo